YORK NOTES

General Editors: Professor A.N. Jeffares (*University of Stirling*) & Professor Suheil Bushrui (*American University of Beirut*)

Samuel Taylor Coleridge

SELECTED POEMS

Notes by Richard Gravil

BA (WALES) PH D (EAST ANGLIA)
Senior Lecturer in English, The College of St Mark and St John

LONGMAN
YORK PRESS

YORK PRESS
Immeuble Esseily, Place Riad Solh, Beirut.

ADDISON WESLEY LONGMAN LIMITED
Edinburgh Gate, Harlow,
Essex CM20 2JE, England
Associated companies, branches and representatives
throughout the world

© Librairie du Liban 1982

First published 1982
Thirteenth impression 1997

ISBN 0-582-03092-7

Produced by Longman Singapore Publishers Pte Ltd
Printed in Singapore

Contents

Part 1

Introduction

Life of Coleridge (1772–1834)

Samuel Taylor Coleridge was born in the Devon village of Ottery St Mary on 21 October 1772, the youngest of ten children in the family of John Coleridge, vicar and schoolmaster. His father died when Coleridge was nine, and in the following year the boy was sent to Christ's Hospital, a famous charity school in London. He was a brilliant pupil, excelling in the classical curriculum and immersing himself at an early age in the study of metaphysics and theology. His lifelong friend, the essayist Charles Lamb (1775–1834), was a fellow pupil.

At the age of nineteen, in October 1791, Coleridge entered Jesus College, Cambridge, and began an erratic career. After two years of successful scholarship, during which he won a prize for poetic composition, his study was interrupted. He was in debt, and his first love, Mary Evans, had rejected him. In December 1793 he left college and enlisted in the army, in the 15th Regiment of Light Dragoons, under the pseudonym of Silas Tomkyn Comberbach. Why an ardent student radical should have joined the army at a time when war with revolutionary France was imminent is only the first of many inexplicable features of Coleridge's career. It was soon noticed, however, that this soldier's Greek was better than his horsemanship, and by the following April his identity was known. After his eldest brother had paid for his release from the regiment, Coleridge returned to the University of Cambridge. He left, finally, in December 1794, without taking a degree—perhaps because the political atmosphere of those days was too exciting to allow him to concentrate on a merely academic course.

In June of that year Coleridge had walked to Oxford, where he met the poet Robert Southey (1774–1843). Together they conceived an idealistic project for emigration to America, to found a commune as an experiment in 'human perfectibility'. Coleridge called the scheme Pantisocracy. Another lifelong friend, Thomas Poole (1765–1837), described the scheme as follows:

> Twelve gentlemen of good education and liberal principles are to embark with twelve ladies in April next. Previous to their leaving this country they are to have as much intercourse as possible, in order to ascertain each other's dispositions, and firmly to settle every regulation for the government of their future conduct....

Each of the men would work for two or three hours a day, 'the produce of which labour would, they imagine, be more than sufficient to support the colony'. Property would be communal, and leisure time would be devoted to reading and philosophical discussion.

In the summer of 1795 the plan collapsed in bitterness, Coleridge accusing Southey of having betrayed his republican principles: apparently he had decided, after all, that servants would be needed in the new society! The friendship, nevertheless, survived this quarrel. The two poets had not only collaborated on the Pantisocracy scheme; they had also written a play together (*The Fall of Robespierre*, 1794), and lived together in Bristol, where Coleridge had given a series of lectures on political events. Besides, they were soon to be related. Robert Southey was engaged to Edith Fricker. In the interests of the Pantisocracy experiment, and despite his attachment to Mary Evans, Coleridge became engaged to Edith's sister, Sara Fricker, whom he married, with some misgivings, in October 1795.

Their married life began happily enough in a cottage at Clevedon in Somerset. Here Coleridge worked hard, writing and editing a political journal, *The Watchman*. Only ten issues were published: there was not a large enough public for a journal both radical and philosophical. When this failed, the Coleridges were helped by Thomas Poole, a prosperous businessman of liberal views, who raised funds to support Coleridge and his family (their first son, David Hartley Coleridge, was born in September 1796), and found for them a cottage at Nether Stowey in the Quantock hills—still known as Coleridge's cottage.

It was here, in the spring of 1797, that Coleridge began his friendship with William Wordsworth and his sister, Dorothy, though he had first met Wordsworth (1770–1850) in 1795. The Wordsworths were living at Racedown, some forty miles away in Dorset, when Coleridge visited them for the first time on 5 June 1797. The magnetic force of this momentous literary friendship was such that the following month the Wordsworths moved into a large house at Alfoxden, only three miles from Stowey, found for them by Thomas Poole. Late in the summer of the following year, 1798, appeared one of the most famous of literary collaborations, the *Lyrical Ballads*. But this product of two great poets needs separate treatment, when we have finished the story of Coleridge's life.

Throughout 1797 Coleridge had been considering his career. he was writing a tragedy, *Osorio* (which was performed successfully only in 1813 under another title, *Remorse*), and contributing articles to a newspaper, *The Morning Post*. In January 1798, after much deliberation, he was preparing to become a minister of the Unitarian Church. He preached a trial sermon in Shrewsbury, to a congregation which included the essayist and critic William Hazlitt (1778–1830), who described the event in 'My First Acquaintance with Poets':

Mr Coleridge rose and gave out his text, 'And he went up into the mountain to pray, HIMSELF, ALONE.' As he gave out this text, his voice 'rose like a steam of rich distilled perfumes'; and when he came to the two last words, which he pronounced loud, deep, and distinct, it seemed to me, who was then young, as if the sounds had echoed from the bottom of the human heart, and as if that prayer might have floated in solemn silence through the universe.

But at this critical point in his career Coleridge was offered an annuity of one hundred and fifty pounds for life, to enable him to concentrate on literature. His patrons were Tom and Josiah Wedgwood, the philanthropic sons of the founder of a famous pottery firm. The early part of 1798 was devoted to poetry, as if in justification of the Wedgwoods' generosity. An outpouring which had begun in 1797 with 'This Lime-tree Bower My Prison' continued with 'The Ancient Mariner', 'Kubla Khan', 'Frost at Midnight', 'France: an Ode', 'The Nightingale', 'Fears in Solitude' and the beginnings of 'Christabel'. All but a handful of his greatest poems belong to this period, the first year of his friendship with Wordsworth.

In May 1798 a second son, Berkeley, was born. He was named, as was Hartley, after one of the philosophers Coleridge most admired at the time. In September, however, Coleridge and the Wordsworths left for Germany. This was perhaps a sensible move for two young radicals who were under observation by the authorities, and who had been visited in 1797 by John Thelwall, a leading radical, much to the alarm of their neighbours. But their ostensible purposes were to perfect their knowledge of the German language, and for Coleridge to study German philosophy and science, which he did at the University of Göttingen until July 1799.

The Wordsworths, on their return to England, stayed for a while with the Hutchinson family near Durham in the North of England. William was to marry Mary Hutchinson in 1802. Coleridge visited them there, and fell in love with Sara Hutchinson, beginning a long relationship which was both sad and inspirational. William and Dorothy settled in Grasmere, in the Lake District, in 1800. For the early part of 1800 Coleridge was in London, reporting parliamentary debates for *The Morning Post* and translating a play, *The Death of Wallenstein*, by the German dramatist and poet J. C. F. von Schiller (1759–1805). Then, although increasingly estranged from his wife, Coleridge brought his family north to live in a fine house, Greta Hall, in Keswick, some fourteen miles from the Wordsworth household at Dove Cottage. The Southey family soon followed, in 1802, to share Greta Hall. When, in 1804, Coleridge left his wife, Southey (who had been partly responsible for the marriage) took over responsibility for looking after his sister-in-law and her children.

At first, Coleridge was happy in the new setting. Greta Hall is a splendid house with magnificent views over England's most beautiful scenery (Keswick, on Derwentwater, is now a popular centre of tourism; in Coleridge's day it was already becoming famous among connoisseurs of the 'sublime and beautiful'). Visits between the Coleridge and Wordsworth households were frequent: from Keswick to Grasmere is a thirteen-mile walk by the direct route, though Coleridge was vigorous enough to cross Helvellyn (3118 feet high) en route on several occasions.

The wet climate, however, did not suit him. Frequent illnesses made him more and more dependent on laudanum (liquid opium) for the relief of pain. Like many of his contemporaries he used this drug for many years and became addicted to it. He was also extending his philosophical and scientific studies in an experimental manner, subjecting himself to 'a multitude of little experiments on my own sensations and on my senses, and some of these (too often repeated) I have reason to believe did injury to my nervous system'. This injurious 'abstruse research' is referred to in the 'dejection poems'.

Worsening health and domestic discord drove him abroad. From June 1804 he was in Malta for two years, acting for a time as secretary to the Governor. But his health was no better, and his spirits were worse, when he returned to London in 1806, via Italy. After eighteen nomadic months, partly in London (where he gave a course of philosophical lectures in January 1808), and partly on visits to friends, he returned to the Lake District. From August 1808 to May 1810 he shared the Wordsworths' home in Grasmere, and with Sara Hutchinson's help produced twenty-seven numbers of his periodical *The Friend*. When Sara left, to live with a brother, Coleridge moved back to Keswick for a time, and then to London, to stay with another old friend, Basil Montagu (whose son had been tutored by the Wordsworths in 1797).

By this time, Coleridge's temperament was a trial to all his friends. In October 1810 he quarrelled with Montagu, who quoted to him Wordsworth's well-meant warning that Coleridge would be difficult to live with; and so began an estrangement from the Wordsworths that lasted eighteen years.

From 1810 to 1816 Coleridge's life was personally ruinous, yet remarkably productive. He gave several courses of lectures, wrote for newspapers, and saw his tragedy performed. He prepared an edition of his poems, and began the composition of his literary autobiography, *Biographia Literaria*.

In April 1816 a medical friend, Dr James Gillman, took charge of Coleridge. For the remainder of his life Coleridge enjoyed the professional and kindly care of Dr and Mrs Gillman whose house-patient he was. Gillman brought both his illness and his addiction under control. The greater part of Coleridge's philosophical and critical writing belongs to this period, including *The Statesman's Manual* (1817), *On Method* (1818) and *Aids to Reflection* (1825).

In 1824 Coleridge was made an associate of the newly established Royal Society of Literature, with a pension of one hundred pounds a year. In 1828 his friendship with Wordsworth was sufficiently revived for them to tour the Rhine together. In that year, too, he published his collected *Poetical Works*, and in 1830 his *On the Constitution of Church and State*.

These late works, especially *Aids to Reflection* and *Church and State*, made Coleridge one of the formative intellectual influences on the rising generation of the great Victorians. He had about him, at meetings in the Gillmans' house, a circle of disciples who came repeatedly to listen to 'the sage of Highgate'. Throughout these years, Coleridge was keen to press on with a great philosophical work, his *magnum opus*. Only fragments were completed in publishable form, but everything Coleridge wrote is related to the central theme of that philosophical project. It was not as the author of a number of books that Coleridge was listened to by the young intellectuals of the time, but as a man who had an unparalleled grasp of the history of philosophy, a deep insight into the philosophical and theological issues of the age, and a gift for inspirational exposition of those problems.

Coleridge died on 25 July 1834, in Highgate, where he is buried. His life had been one of suffering, and by the standard of his own ambitions he had achieved very little. Yet his death was felt as a deep loss. It was natural that Wordsworth should remember him as 'the most wonderful man I have ever known', and that Lamb should feel: 'Never saw I his likeness, nor probably the world can see again'. But others, too, felt deprived of a great intellectual presence. In 1838 John Stuart Mill (1806–73), greatest of the Utilitarian philosophers, wrote of Coleridge— whose thought was radically different from his own—as one of the two 'great seminal minds' of the age.

The friendship with Wordsworth

All statements about Coleridge's life should be viewed with the greatest suspicion. Despite the attentions of generations of scholars even the details of his biography are open to dispute. Some say that he fell in love with Sara Hutchinson in 1799; others deny that his feelings were deeply engaged before 1802. Was he an ardent revolutionary as a student? The evidence is confused, and endlessly disputed. His military pseudonym is spelt Comberbach, Comberbache, Comberback and Comberbacke, by equally reputable scholars. And although the facts about his friendship with Wordsworth are not greatly disputed, the interpretations of those facts agree on only one point: that this was one of the most productive friendships in literary history.

Wordsworth published in 1793 two long poems, *An Evening Walk* and *Descriptive Sketches*. Both were read and admired by Coleridge. When they first met, in Bristol in 1795, Coleridge was lecturing on political affairs. 'I saw but little of him,' said Wordsworth. 'I wished indeed to have seen more—his talent appears to me very great.' By the next spring they were corresponding with each other: Wordsworth sent his next long poem, 'Salisbury Plain', to Coleridge for criticism—a mark of great respect, and of confidence in Coleridge's sympathy. In May, Coleridge was already calling Wordsworth 'a very dear friend of mine, the best poet of the age', which judgement was no doubt influenced by the fact that Wordsworth had admired Coleridge's 'Religious Musings', published in 1795. Some time in 1796 Wordsworth read aloud to Coleridge part of 'Salisbury Plain'. As Coleridge recorded many years later:

> ... while memory lasts, I shall hardly forget the sudden effect produced on my mind. ... It was not however the freedom from false taste, whether as to common defects, or to those more properly his own, which made so unusual an impression on my feelings immediately and subsequently on my judgement. It was the union of deep feeling with profound thought ... and above all the original gift of spreading the tone, the atmosphere ... of the ideal world around forms, incidents and situations of which, for the common view, custom had bedimmed all the lustre. (*Biographia Literaria*, Chapter 4)

By April 1797 the two poets were each engaged in writing a tragedy— Wordsworth's *The Borderers* and Coleridge's *Osorio*—and were agreed in their critial view of Southey's poetry, that it was written 'too much at his ease'. In July they became neighbours.

What are we to make of this collision? One view is that Wordsworth, a dour Northerner, who had written a quantity of rather dull verse in eighteenth-century style, suddenly found a friend whose brilliant mind gave him new themes and a new style. Coleridge gave Wordsworth his most elevated theme, that of 'the one Life within us and abroad', and, by inventing (in 'This Lime-tree Bower' and other poems) a new mode of 'conversational' poetry, he gave Wordsworth the new style of his greater poems. Without the encouragement and inspiration of Coleridge, Wordsworth could never have written 'Tintern Abbey' and *The Prelude*. Yet Wordsworth returned such generous gifts with coolness, unable to recognise the genius of Coleridge's poetry: 'the poem of my friend has indeed great defects', was Wordsworth's famous comment on 'The Ancient Mariner'. Wordsworth blindly accepted Coleridge's humble estimate of their respective merits, and helped to magnify Coleridge's self-doubts. As Coleridge wrote to William Godwin in 1801, Wordsworth 'by showing to him what true poetry was' made Coleridge know 'that he himself was no Poet'. As their friendship failed, however, so did Wordsworth's poetry. Wordsworth was Coleridge's creation, claimed one influential critic, and like all his works he left it unfinished.

Another view suggests that Wordsworth did indeed show Coleridge what true poetry was. When they became close friends, Wordsworth was already at the peak of his powers. He had written by mid-1797 not only 'Salisbury Plain', which had so powerfully struck Coleridge, but one of his greatest pieces, 'The Ruined Cottage', which Coleridge later described as the finest poem of its length in the English language. Coleridge, on the other hand, had written only juvenile pieces and the long 'Religious Musings' which, like his other reflective poems, is in a conventional style heavily influenced by the seventeenth-century poet John Milton (1608–74). Until Coleridge met William and Dorothy Wordsworth he had no 'eye' for nature, and it was Wordsworth who gave him a fresh poetic voice, free from abstractions and conventional imagery.

Both of these views have many supporters—for each of these poets is loved by his readers to the point of jealous and fierce rivalry. It takes an effort of detachment to look at the matter coolly, but if the effort is made it may be seen as follows. In 1797 two rising poets became neighbours and firm friends. Like most friendships, theirs was based on enough affinity and enough diversity between the friends to mean that Wordsworth and Coleridge, for many years, gave each other the kind of support they needed. Coleridge had the finest audience a young philosopher could have—doggedly sceptical and hard to convince, but willing to let his brilliant friend talk away, unimpeded. Wordsworth had an admirer who not only saw him as a great poet in the line of Edmund Spenser (1552–99), William Shakespeare (1564–1616) and John Milton, but who could produce critical theories to prove it. With such generous support, Wordsworth was able to survive years of critical incomprehension and hostility. In the presence of the Wordsworth household—a 'family of love', they were called—Coleridge found the inspiration to produce most of his finest poetry, and much (in the essays of *The Friend*) of his early philosophical writing.

Coleridge and his times

The adult life of Coleridge spans the historical period from the French Revolution of 1789 to the First Reform Bill of 1832. When Coleridge was seventeen, the Bastille prison was stormed by crowds in Paris; when he was twenty-one King Louis XVI was executed, as was the despotic revolutionary leader, Robespierre, a year later. He was thirty-two when Napoleon became Emperor, and forty-three when the Duke of Wellington and Marshal Blücher defeated Napoleon at the Battle of Waterloo. He was forty-seven when in 1819 an English crowd demanding the reform of Parliament was fired upon by mounted soldiers: this incident, the Peterloo Massacre, was a formative event in the lives of the next generation of Romantic poets, Lord Byron (1788–1824) then thirty-one years old, Percy Bysshe Shelley (1792–1822) and John Keats (1795–1821). The partial reformation of parliamentary franchise in England (the reform of constituencies and extension of the vote) was enacted when Coleridge was sixty. In the last year of his life, 1833–4, Parliament passed an Act preventing the employment of children under the age of nine, and another establishing the hated system of 'workhouses' for the poor; slavery was abolished in the British Empire, and a group of Dorsetshire labourers, the Tolpuddle Martyrs, were transported to Australia for illegally joining a trade union. The age, one might conclude, began with clear-cut revolutionary issues and ended in a muddle of contradictory legislation. Coleridge, who began his political life by supporting the French Revolution and ended it in opposing the Reform Bill, may seem at first to share this muddle.

For a whole generation of young English writers the dominant fact of the early 1790s was, as Wordsworth expressed it in *The Prelude*:

France standing on the top of golden hours
And human nature seeming born again.

If there were any young writers who did not share that enthusiasm, they have been forgotten. Edmund Burke, representing a conservative constitutional position, published his *Reflections on the Revolution in France* in 1790, but his eloquence had no effect, at the time, on Coleridge's generation. In 1791, the year Coleridge entered Cambridge, Thomas Paine's *The Rights of Man* was published, to answer Burke's criticisms and to argue for the establishment of a republic in England— by revolutionary means if necessary. This work, which sold one and a half million copies, is still a classic of radical thought: it helped to create a political opposition so fervent and articulate that the government of the day resorted to savage measures of repression. In 1793 William Godwin published his *Inquiry Concerning Political Justice*. Godwin, a friend of Coleridge, Wordsworth and Shelley, took a more philosophical approach, but his work is equally radical in its vision of the just society which it prophesied as the inevitable result of the evolution of man's reason.

Increasingly, however, the poets found themselves having to distinguish between revolutionary ideals and revolutionary practice. The

'September Massacres' of the French nobility, the execution of the King, the 'Reign of Terror' under Robespierre—in which thousands were guillotined—and the ruling Directory's acts of war against the Netherlands and the Rhineland, were a chain of events which dismayed the English radicals. Nevertheless, when war was declared between England and France in February 1793, Wordsworth, Coleridge and their friends were still essentially in sympathy with France. Both had friends who were imprisoned in 1794 on charges of treason, and they themselves wrote articles for which they could have been arrested.

Wordsworth, who visited revolutionary France in 1790, and lived there for a year in 1791–2, retained his sympathy with the revolution until 1802 (the date of France's second invasion of Switzerland); perhaps even until 1804, when Napoleon—who had replaced Robespierre as dictator—was crowned Emperor. Coleridge's disillusion was more rapid. By 1798 he had clearly recanted his revolutionary views. His poetic disavowal in 'France: an Ode' was written in February 1798, immediately following the first invasion of Switzerland. In April he wrote to his brother: 'I have snapped my squeaking baby trumpet of sedition . . . I wish to be a good man and a Christian, but I am no Whig, no Reformist, no Republican'. Since the 'Whigs' were by no means radical—we should now call them the party of bourgeois liberalism—this statement aligns Coleridge firmly with conservative opinion. He goes on: 'I have for some time past withdrawn myself totally from the consideration of *immediate causes*, which are infinitely complex and uncertain, to muse on fundamental and general causes'.

Such a tendency was apparent in Coleridge's thought as early as 1795. When he lectured in Bristol he certainly had the reputation of a Jacobin—a revolutionary enthusiast—but his published lecture is in fact a philosophical consideration of the violent excesses of revolution. 'French freedom,' he says, 'is the beacon which if it guides us to equality should show us likewise the dangers that throng the road.' The French 'hastened into the gigantic error of making certain evil the means of contingent [that is, uncertain] good'. Robespierre's aim was not necessarily wicked: 'I rather think, that the distant prospect, to which he was travelling, appeared to him grand and beautiful; but that he fixed his eye on it with such intense eagerness as to neglect the foulness of the road.' Such power as Robespierre possessed 'shapes and depraves the character of the possessor'. The conclusion which Coleridge draws from the example of Robespierre finely expresses the appalling connection between political idealism and political crime:

If we clearly perceive any one thing to be of vast and infinite importance to ourselves and all mankind, our first feelings impel us to turn with angry contempt from those who doubt and oppose it. The ardour of undisciplined benevolence seduces us into malignity: and whenever our hearts are warm, and our objects great and excellent, intolerance is the sin that does most easily beset us.

The lecture (published in *The Friend*, Essay XVI) makes clear that Coleridge is by no means a revolutionary in 1795. He goes on to reject any political philosophy which casts doubt on the value of primary human affections:

Let us beware of that proud philosophy which affects to inculcate philanthropy while it denounces every home-born feeling by which it is produced and nurtured. The paternal and filial duties discipline the heart and prepare it for the love of all mankind. The intensity of private attachments encourages, not prevents, universal benevolence.

'Benevolence' is a term associated with Godwin's *Political Justice*. Twice in this lecture Coleridge casts doubt on the term, first as something which can mislead us into malignity, and secondly as having no validity unless it is a natural outgrowth from private attachments, which Godwin thought were the root of social evil.

Ironically, then, the only extant prose work of Coleridge in which he is supposedly defending the revolution is already an exposition of a quietist, if not conservative, philosophy. For a time, however, Coleridge continued to mix with radical circles. His journalism in 1796–7 is still strongly anti-government. Yet his instincts were, unlike Wordsworth's, fundamentally conservative even at this time. His poem 'Fears in Solitude', written in April 1798 when a French invasion was feared, is more patriotic than revolutionary. But Coleridge never became an unthinking patriot. His concern, in this poem, is whether his country *deserves* its liberty. He sees it as guilty of tyranny, polluted by the quest of wealth, and foolishly clamouring for war. His countrymen are divided between naïve radicals who expect 'all change from change of constituted power', and 'idolators' who react to all events with baseless pride in British institutions. Three years later (in a letter of 23 March 1801 to Thomas Poole) he is still contemplating emigration to America — not in search of utopia, but out of disgust with 'the state of my poor oppressed country' where 'the laborious poor are dying with grass in their bellies'. He laments 'our pestilent commerce, our unnatural crowding together of men in cities, and our government by rich men'.

For the first three decades of the nineteenth century England suffered the consequences of the Napoleonic Wars. Democratic institutions had been undermined by the Government's war dictatorship. The growing cities of the Industrial Revolution were overcrowded with working families whose livelihood was threatened by mechanisation. The rule of commercial interests, with their belief in a *laissez-faire* economic theory (that market forces should determine economic policy), was creating appalling working and living conditions for the new proletariat and the old peasantry. When the war ended, the returning soldiers raised the already insufferable level of unemployment, and there was a decade or more of industrial unrest.

In this situation most radicals began to campaign energetically for parliamentary reform, to extend the franchise to the population of the new industrial cities, and to abolish the 'rotten boroughs' where parliamentary constituencies still existed in depopulated rural areas and the Member of Parliament was in effect chosen by the local nobleman.

That Coleridge was not in sympathy with this movement may seem strange. He was, however, disturbed by three elements in the reform movement. First, he felt that it would increase, rather than diminish, the power of commercial interests in Parliament—at the expense of traditional interests, such as the Church of England and the landed aristocracy, which had, he believed, a more disinterested view of good government. 'The enormous aggregation of capital,' he said in his *Table Talk*, was one of the country's chief economic ills. Secondly, he found the Reform Bill's supporters guilty of crimes against rational argument: 'the arguments of its advocates, and the manner of their advocacy, are a thousand times worse than the Bill itself' (*Table Talk*, 20 November 1831). Thirdly, he was in deep disagreement with the Utilitarian social philosophy of the liberal reformers.

What he wished to see was not a parliament representative of the clamorous new industrial areas, carrying out 'the will of the people', but one which would truly represent the 'Idea of the State'. In his work *The Constitution of Church and State* he gives an account of that 'Idea'. In its ideal form, the state is a balance of 'permanence' and 'progression', or of the 'landed interest' of the aristocracy and gentry on the one hand, and the representatives of manufacturers, merchants and the professions on the other. While it was true that the interests of permanence were better represented than those of progression in the unreformed Parliament, the reform movement was not, in Coleridge's view, likely to amend matters. For in his 'Idea of the State' there is a third component, concerned not with permanence or progression but with 'cultivation': this component Coleridge calls a 'National Church' and the 'Clerisy'—that is, those whose functions are above all spiritual and educational, and whose contribution to national government is the pursuit of civilisation in its broadest sense. This group, ideally, owes loyalty neither to any existing party nor to pursuit of material wealth, but to the best possible realisation of the spiritual ends of the nation. Since the reform movement was unlikely to realise Coleridge's 'Idea' of what the State ought to be, Coleridge could not support it. Political change for its own sake, and without an adequate 'Idea', was useless, and usually harmful.

Through Coleridge's apparent political instability runs a constant thread, that of Christian Platonism. His Pantisocracy scheme was in effect a plan for a group of Christian gentlemen to establish Plato's ideal Republic in miniature. He favoured the French Revolution for as long as could persuade himself that it was guided by an adequate 'Idea'. In his conservative phase, for instance in *Church and State*, such idealism (essentially a philosophical idealism) is still present. Coleridge's political thought is always radical, in the sense of being concerned with the root of the matter: that it ceases to take a radical (in the sense of left-wing) position does not mean that Coleridge changed his fundamental principles.

Coleridge's work

What, essentially, was Coleridge? Many readers see him as primarily a great poet, whose poetic output was sadly diminished, even stifled, by an unfortunate taste for philosophy. To others he was essentially a philosopher, who happened to have brilliant poetic gifts. Others see him as a man of immense and varied talents who frittered away his life in a series of brilliant gestures—in poetry, journalism, political and religious writings—and left no substantial work in any of these fields. In part, Coleridge created this myth of himself as a creature of fits and starts but disappointing achievement.

Yet even the work completed and published in his lifetime was impressive in its scope. He published a substantial body of poetry, including a number of the finest poems in the language. His *Biographia Literaria* (1817) is not merely an autobiography but a work of philosophical and critical influence. Apart from his periodicals, *The Watchman* and *The Friend*, he published four works on religion and political theory, *The Statesman's Manual, A Lay Sermon, Aids to Reflection*, and *The Constitution of Church and State*. In his lifetime he was celebrated both as a journalist and as a lecturer, and for his letters and his conversation. From these sources several generations of scholars have edited the following posthumous works: *The Collected Letters*, edited by E. L. Griggs, in six volumes; *Table Talk; Confessions of an Inquiring Spirit* and *Anima Poetae* (selections from his notebooks); *The Philosophical Lectures* and *Shakespearean Criticism*; and two distinguished philosophical essays, *Treatise on Method* and *A Theory of Life*.

In addition to these twenty volumes, Coleridge left some seventy notebooks containing his thoughts on an immense range of subjects; *The Notebooks of Samuel Taylor Coleridge*, edited by Kathleen Coburn, fill five bulky double volumes. A reconstruction of his great work of philosophical synthesis, from which all his other activities were lifelong distractions, is now being edited.

The range and quantity of Coleridge's work are far beyond the reach of men as 'indolent' as Coleridge said he was. But the unity of that work is perhaps harder to see.

In a letter to Sir Humphrey Davy (1778–1829), the scientist, in February 1801, Coleridge made a remarkable statement which shows how he saw one aspect of his work in the context of the whole. He was planning to write a work 'Concerning Poetry and the nature of the Pleasures derived from it', and he comments: 'I am sure that if I write what I ought to do on it, the work would supersede all the books of metaphysics, and all the books of morals too'. That is an astonishing claim, but Coleridge is only half joking. All his works in literary criticism, philosophy, theology and political theory—and all his notebook jottings on topics from philology to psychology—relate to a constant philosophical project, which was to affirm man's spiritual nature, and to demonstrate moral freedom and the creativity of the imagination. For Coleridge, no kind of human enquiry could be seen as unrelated to the illumination of the nature of human life, and to answering the great questions of philosophy to which all research into the humanities or the natural sciences must finally contribute. These questions, he said in his *Philosophical Lectures*, are 'what and *for* what am I made? what *can* I and what *ought* I to make of myself? and in what relations do I stand to the world and to my fellow men?'

A note on the text

Coleridge's poems were published in various volumes: *Poems on Various Subjects* (1796), *Lyrical Ballads* (1798), *Sybilline Leaves* (1817) and *Poetical Works* (1828). The standard edition is *The Complete Poetical Works of Samuel Taylor Coleridge*, edited by E. H. Coleridge, Oxford University Press, Oxford, 1912. All of the poems discussed in these notes are included in *Coleridge: Poems*, edited by John Beer, Everyman's Library, J. M. Dent, London, 1974, which is the edition quoted in these notes. All except the 'Letter to Sara Hutchinson' are in *The Portable Coleridge*, edited by I. A. Richards, The Viking Press, New York, 1950; Penguin Books, Harmondsworth, 1977.

Part 2

Summaries
of SELECTED POEMS BY
COLERIDGE

THE POEMS ARE SUMMARISED in approximate chronological order.

Sonnet: To the River Otter (1793)

Coleridge apostrophises the Otter, the stream which gives its name to his birth-place, Ottery St Mary. His reminiscences of the appearance of the stream, and the pleasures he associates with it, are blended with references to his present state of manhood. One particular memory, that of skimming flat stones along the surface of the water counting how many times they bounce, opens the poem. So great was the pleasure of this activity, it is implied, that whenever in later years the poet closes his eyes on a sunlit scene the waters of the Otter rise in memory. The syntax of lines 11–13 is best read as: 'Often on my way (through life) such visions of childhood have soothed the cares of manhood, and they still make me fondly sigh. . . .'

NOTES AND GLOSSARY:
river, brook, streamlet: each term is more diminutive
the West: the counties of Devon, Cornwall, Somerset and Dorset are together known as the West Country
imprest: impressed
marge: margin, bank
vein'd with various dyes: a reference to the different colours of the rock strata which have contributed to the sandy bed of the river
yet: still

The Eolian Harp (August 1795)

The Aeolian (or Eolian) harp was a seventeenth-century invention. It was a musical instrument consisting of tuned strings stretched over a sounding-box. Aeolus was god of the winds: the harp was placed in a window where it responded to the changing breeze with sequences of chords, as though Aeolus were playing it. Coleridge represents himself and Sara Fricker, a few weeks before their marriage, sitting in their garden at dusk and listening to this music—the music of nature. Their cottage has climbing plants, emblematic of innocence and love. The clouds, losing their light, are 'slow(ly) saddening (a)round (us)', and the scene is quiet enough for the distant sea to be heard.

The lute, or harp, clasped by the casement window, is first described as emblematic of a yielding maid, reproving her lover—the caressing wind. Then it suggests, more fancifully, the bewitching sounds of elves, and melodies which seem to hover like birds of paradise. Lines 26–33 were added to the poem in 1817: they express Coleridge's occasional sense of the harmony between the soul and all creation—'O! the one Life within us and abroad'—in which joy is the common element of all life, and even the 'still air/ Is music slumbering. . . .'

'And thus, my love'—that is, just as the wind plays its harp—various thoughts and fantasies cross the poet's brain, as he idly watches the sun's reflections on the distant sea at noon. Such thoughts come and go like the natural breeze. One such thought now comes to him: what if all life is subject in the same way to 'one intellectual breeze/ At once the Soul of each, and God of all?'

The sudden change in the poem at line 49 may seem inexplicable. The idea of God's presence in nature is an attractive one, after all. But Coleridge identifies it immediately as a Pantheistic thought, and therefore a heresy: in the orthodox Christian view, God is not to be confused with his creation. So the final verse paragraph makes amends for the idle heresy with numerous expressions of orthodox piety. The poet feels reproved by Sara's eye—and perhaps her tongue. Her meekness, mildness and humility as a 'Daughter of Christ' show his own thoughts to be 'dim and unhallowed' (unholy). He rejects his fine thought as a creation of the 'unregenerate mind' and of the ever-babbling spring of vain philosophy. He may not identify God with his own soul: rather he gives thanks for God's gifts—salvation (without which he would be lost in sin and bewilderment), peace, his cottage, and Sara.

Outbursts of piety in Coleridge's poems are frequent. Readers may feel more impressed by the beauty of the Pantheistic thought than by the orthodox faith to which the poem returns. But the poem expresses a genuine intellectual drama in which Coleridge's deeply speculative mind finds itself in conflict with his Christian faith. Perhaps the excessively pious language of the close is a sign of how powerfully he is tempted by Pantheism. There is also something of a return to the mood of quiet thankfulness with which the poem opens—a characteristic pattern in Coleridge's meditative poems.

NOTES AND GLOSSARY:

Pantheism: see p.54 of these notes
cot: cottage

Jasmin(e) and Myrtle: climbing shrubs, both with aromatic white flowers

casement: window

sequacious: successive

the Main: poetic term for the sea

plastic: forming, moulding

unregenerate: unreformed, unspiritual

aye babbling: talking incessantly and foolishly (though often used to describe the sound of springs or streams)

wilder'd: bewildered, both in the sense of 'mentally confused', and in the older sense of 'exiled into wilderness'

Reflections on Having Left a Place of Retirement (1795)

For business reasons, relating to the publication of his poems and his preparations for editing *The Watchman*, Coleridge found it necessary to move to Bristol. This poem records his feelings on leaving the cottage at Clevedon, where he had felt 'the unobtrusive song of Happiness'. There, too, by climbing a steep path, he could attain a wider view of the world about him—the ascent, of course, is allegorical of the efforts required, and the discomforts involved, in achieving a universal outlook. Some peotic licence is employed, in that there is certainly no 'bare bleak mountain' anywhere near Clevedon.

A distant view of humanity, however, whether from the domestic tranquillity of the cottage or from the sublime solitude of the mountain, is not what the political situation requires of him. Behind Coleridge's rather abstract meditation on the superiority of real brotherhood to either cold benevolence or refined pity, lies his sense that he should be sharing the dangers faced by fellow radicals who were labouring in the cities, trying to defend civil liberties against an increasingly repressive government. It would be cowardly to stay in Clevedon nursing his conscience, instead of committing himself to the political arena. In the event it was as a journalist that he went to Bristol, 'Active and firm, to fight the bloodless fight/ Of Science, Freedom, and the Truth in Christ': the causes of liberty, religious truth, and philosophical enquiry were, for Coleridge, one and the same.

The poem returns at the close to the image of the cottage, but now as an emblem of a better future in which all men will be able to enjoy such idyllic conditions as he now sacrifices—a future in which all men will be equal in God's earthly kingdom. Although in this poem Coleridge uses his habitual capitalised abstract nouns—Commerce, Pity, Wretchedness—the feeling is genuine. Especially powerful is another instance of Coleridge's sense of a divine presence in nature—'It seem'd like Omnipresence....'

NOTES AND GLOSSARY:

Bristowa's citizen: a citizen of Bristol
viewless: unseen
dell: small wooded valley
the Channel: the Bristol Channel (the dim coasts are those of Wales)

The Dungeon (1797)

This brief extract from Act 5 of Coleridge's tragedy *Osorio* was first printed in *Lyrical Ballads* as a self-sufficient poem. The theme of captivity was a powerful one in the Romantic era—compare Byron's famous poem 'The Prisoner of Chillon', or the prison setting of the great opera *Fidelio* by Beethoven (1770–1827). Perhaps the storming of that hated French prison, the Bastille, accounts for this obsessive theme, but it is a natural counterpoint to the theme of liberty. Here the grim portrayal of dark captivity is counterpointed in the second part by joyful celebration of liberty. The contrast recalls the most famous thought of the French philosopher Jean-Jacques Rousseau (1712–78): 'Man is born free but everywhere is in chains'. Certainly, prisons are presented here as the work of man, and liberty as the law of nature.

Coleridge's interest is psychological rather than political. He observes the corrupting effects of imprisonment—stagnation, poison, deformity—contrasted with the healing ministry of nature. Nature's music is again stressed. Its melodies and minstrelsy are contrasted with the groaning and clanking sounds of the prison. But the poem does not merely contrast one state with another. It considers nature as a redemptive force, actively healing and reclaiming an erring man, while imprisonment is equally active, able to corrupt even the innocent. Nature is the true healer, while the cure proposed by the 'mountebanks' who put people in prison is worse than the disease. The poem is characteristically Romantic in its overt association of repression with evil.

NOTES AND GLOSSARY:

mountebank: a charlatan or quack-doctor, ignorant of what he teaches

This Lime-tree Bower My Prison (1797)

Our transition here from Dungeon to Prison is purely coincidental, yet there is a point to be made. In this poem Coleridge finds himself confined to the open prison of his neighbour's garden, while his friend Charles Lamb (to whom the poem is addressed) is, in Coleridge's view at least,

enjoying a brief liberation from the great city. The occasion of the poem
is described by Coleridge in a letter to Southey:

> Charles Lamb has been with me for a week—he left me Friday
> morning. The second day after Wordsworth came to me, dear Sara
> accidentally emptied a skillet of boiling milk on my foot, which
> confined me during the whole time of Lamb's stay and still prevents
> me from all walks longer than a furlong. While Wordsworth, his sister,
> and C. Lamb were out one evening; sitting in the arbour of T. Poole's
> garden, which communicates with mine, I wrote these lines, with
> which I am pleased.

The disappointment expressed in the opening lines is very intense:
Coleridge is missing a walk amid much-loved scenery with one of his
oldest friends and two of his newest. Having told them to visit a
particular spot ('that still roaring dell, of which I told'), he follows them
in imagination, recreating the scene in precise detail, and participating
imaginatively in their enjoyment. An entry in Dorothy Wordsworth's
journal describes the same scene in winter: 'Walked to . . . the waterfall.
The adder's-tongue and the ferns green in the low damp dell. These
plants now in perpetual motion from the current of the air; in summer
only moved by the drippings of the rocks.' Adder's-tongue is the name of
the 'long lank weeds' (line 17).

Emerging from the shade, his friends will rejoice in the distant view of
the sea. Imagining Lamb in this scene, Coleridge desires for him a rich
sunset, for his friend is in need of the restorative joy that accompanies
such sights. But in desiring an experience of sublimity for Lamb,
Coleridge himself is overcome by joy, which now spills over into the
scene where he sits 'imprisoned'. The bower itself is filled with radiance,
and with interest, in consequence of his own sense of joy. The moralising
note is less obtrusive in this poem than in 'The Eolian Harp' or
'Reflections', although it is present in lines 64–7 (and perhaps in his
choice of the 'humble-bee' to illustrate contented nature in line 58).

In its subtle and convincing shifts of feeling, and its use of natural,
colloquial speech rhythms, this is the first of Coleridge's wholly
successful 'conversation poems'. It is relatively free of the conventional
emblems and allegory used in his earlier poems, and of formal 'poetic
diction'. There is, however, an awkward double-negative in lines 45–6
('nor . . . have I not marked'), and the imperatives addressed to nature in
lines 32–7 ('richlier burn, ye clouds!', etc.) are too formally rhetorical to
suit the new conversational style of the rest of the poem.

At the close of the poem Coleridge and Lamb are pleasingly united by
the homeward flight of the 'last rook' at evening. The act of 'blessing' the
rook may remind you of the similar event in 'The Ancient Mariner': here
the 'creaking' of the rook's feathers contributes to the harmony of the

scene for those whose hearts are 'awake to Love and Beauty', and to whom 'No sound is dissonant which tells of Life'.

NOTES AND GLOSSARY:

bower: space enclosed by leafy vegetation, arbour

springy: 'elastic, I mean', said Coleridge in a letter to Southey

ash: ash-tree

The many-steepled tract magnificent: the style of this phrase, describing an expanse of countryside in which there are many church steeples, is an example of Coleridge's frequent Miltonisms—imitations of the dignified, sonorous style of John Milton, author of *Paradise Lost*

some fair bark: in poetic diction a 'bark' may be any kind of boat, but technically it is a three-masted sailing vessel

evil and pain/ And strange calamity: the previous year, in a fit of insanity, Charles's sister Mary had stabbed their mother to death. Charles, too, had periods of mental instability, although he was normally the gayest and most gentle of Coleridge's friends

usurps: encroaches upon

no plot so narrow . . .: that is, no plot of ground is too narrow and no waste ground is too empty to stimulate the senses, as long as nature is present

---

Frost at Midnight (February 1798)

Most readers find this the most satisfying of Coleridge's 'conversation poems', for its perfect but unobtrusive form, its subtlety of thought and feeling, and its richness of imagery. Like 'This Lime-tree Bower', this poem has a precise situation. Coleridge is speaking as a parent. His child, Hartley (now about eighteen months old) is sleeping, and in the context of a delicately sketched night scene Coleridge pursues a train of thought. His reverie combines a fascination with his own alert sensibility—attuned to the sharp quietness of the night—with parental concern and hope for the future sensibility of his child.

The frost is a potent opening image. The sharp, clear sounds of the first line (the 'fr', 'st', 'f', 's', 't', 'str' sequence) evoke the sharpness of the night; we are asked to listen, as it were, to the workings of a windless frost, to strain our senses to observe that silent operation of nature—which silence heightens 'the owlet's cry'. The calmness is tangible, vexing the poet's meditation. The 'goings-on of life' are 'inaudible as dreams'. Even the flame of the fire is still. Two things only are 'unquiet': a film of soot flutters on the grate, and in its responsiveness to the otherwise imperceptible currents of air it is felt by the poet as an image for his own 'unquiet' soul.

The 'film' takes him back to his own childhood, when he believed in the superstition that this phenomenon foretold a visitor, so that he would spend the night and the following day in anticipation. If, as often happened, he was already thinking of home, he would expect the 'stranger' to be a visitor from his home-place.

The phrase 'Dear Babe' recalls us to the poet's present situation and feelings, but also links the poet's childhood with his son's. He now looks forward to Hartley's boyhood, as he has looked back on his own, and prophesies that Hartley's will be very different—not 'pent' (imprisoned) among cloisters in the city, but free as a breeze to roam the countryside. The imagery of lakes, shores and crags suggests that Coleridge's thoughts are turning toward Wordsworth's country. Indeed he is foretelling a childhood for Hartley which owes much to Wordsworth's recollections of his own. In lines 55–8 Coleridge repeats certain terms to imitate the way in which the clouds imitate the landscape below. Again, a strong current of feeling leads Coleridge to associate the 'lovely shapes and sounds' of nature with the language of God.

The last movement, or verse paragraph, imagines the seasons to come, summers alternating with winters; but the imagery returns us gradually to the present scene—the snow, the thatch, the silences when the wind is in a trance—preparing us for the beautiful repetition of the opening image, that 'secret ministry' of frost hanging up the water drops in 'silent icicles/ Quietly shining to the quiet Moon'. The ministry of natural forces is now understood more deeply, however, in the light of the third movement, as both natural and divine. The icicles and the moon are more closely connected than appears on the surface: the icicles, shining 'to' the moon, are reflecting the moon's reflected light, and so are mysteriously linked in a chain of reflections from the life-giving sun.

NOTES AND GLOSSARY:

vexes:	usually 'annoys', but here 'stirs' or 'moves'
freaks:	caprices, vagaries
presageful:	full of presentiments
preceptor:	*(archaic)* teacher
playmate ... clothed alike:	that is, when both wore baby-clothes
lore:	teaching, traditional wisdom
redbreast:	robin (a favourite bird in the English winter scene)

France: an Ode (February 1798)

This poem, originally called 'Recantation', was directly inspired by the French invasion of Switzerland. In some editions it is prefaced by

Coleridge's own prose summary, or argument—a helpful device since after the easy flow of 'Frost at Midnight' this poem is made obscure and rather forbidding by its excited rhetoric. The first stanza, Coleridge explains, is 'an invocation to those objects in Nature the contemplation of which had inspired the Poet with a devotional love of Liberty'. The catalogue of images is conventional enough—clouds roll, birds sing, plants flower—except in that Coleridge addresses them (line 18) as 'everything that is and will be free', and calls on them as witnesses to his own worship of liberty.

The second stanza recalls how the poet rejoiced at the French Revolution, and how he was 'unawed' by the disapproval of the 'slavish band' of other Englishmen. When the monarchical powers of Europe, including Britain, tried to crush the revolution, even his patriotic feelings (32–5) did not prevent him supporting the French. 'My voice, unaltered, sang defeat' to the enemies of France. Here Coleridge seems to be identifying himself with the brave and lonely Milton, who said in *Paradise Lost*, 'I sing ... unchanged' after the collapse of the English Revolution in 1660.

The third stanza claims that he looked on the blasphemies and other horrors of the Reign of Terror as a passing storm, behind which the Sun of Liberty was rising. Although he was made anxious by the warlike appearance of France (her 'front deep-scarred and gory' while she crushed 'domestic treason'), he still hoped that France would peacefully compel other nations to be free. In the fourth stanza, however, he refers to the French invasion of Switzerland (Helvetia), and begs Freedom and the Swiss to forgive him for ever having 'blessed your cruel foes'. France has invaded the very home of peace, patriotism and liberty, and has become as bad as the worst of kings.

True liberty, the final stanza says, cannot be found in revolutions led by 'the Sensual and the Dark'. Liberty lives neither with the minions of Priestcraft nor with the slaves of Blasphemy (that is, Catholicism or Atheism). As Coleridge's own summary explains, the ideal of Freedom, which 'the mind attains by its contemplation of its individual nature [the creative liberty of the mind] and of the sublime surrounding objects [the works of nature], does not belong to men, as a society'. Nor can liberty be realised 'under any form of human government'. Liberty belongs only 'to the individual man ... inflamed with the love and adoration of God in Nature'.

NOTES AND GLOSSARY:
gratulation: congratulation
whelm: overwhelm
the tyrant-quelling lance: that is, the lance of the revolution
paeans: songs of thanksgiving

front:	forehead
ramp:	fortification
toils:	snares
sway:	rule
Sensual ... Dark:	those limited to their senses, unenlightened by intellect
Priestcraft's harpy minions:	rapacious (greedy) servants of the priesthood
pinions:	wing feathers

Fears in Solitude (April 1798)

Written, as the sub-title says, 'during the alarm of an invasion', this poem is a meditation composed of observations of nature, anxieties about the possibility of a French invasion, strong criticism of the spiritual state of the nation, patriotic feelings, and thoughts on the meaning of liberty. Although a longer poem, it has something of the circular structure of the conversation poems of 1797–8, beginning and ending with reference to Coleridge's quiet life at Nether Stowey.

Lines 1–28: The poet takes delight in describing his dwelling-place, his 'spirit-healing nook', and how it is loved by all, but especially by such men as can enjoy 'influences' from the lark, the sun and the breeze, making out of these a 'meditative joy' and finding 'Religious Meanings in the forms of Nature' (the man described is partly Coleridge himself, and partly Wordsworth).

Lines 29–86: His calmness is disturbed by thoughts of his fellow men and the possibility that some are already engaged in repelling an invasion. He sees this possibility as too well deserved by a country which has itself invaded others, and whose ruling institutions are a club for 'mutual flattery'. The land is polluted by wealth and forgetful of the true meaning of Christianity. God has been forgotten (and Coleridge is performing the role of a biblical prophet).

Lines 86–129: The nation is guilty of having welcomed war with France, as long as the fighting is done abroad. Even women and children find the news of war exciting, and seem unaware of its cruel realities, 'As if the soldier died without a wound'. What if Providence should decide to teach these thoughtless people the meaning of the words they use so lightly?

Lines 129–52: But the poet prays that they will be spared, and calls on his countrymen to repel the 'impious foe'. Whatever the wickedness of the British, the French have no right to invade. Let the British win, he asks, but not in 'drunken triumph', rather in a spirit of repentance.

Lines 153–74: The true courage his country needs is to look at its own vices, and at the political strife which divides people into two camps— naïve radicals who blame all social ills on the government, and the ruling class who call their critics traitors.

Lines 175–97: He has been called a traitor himself, but here he refutes the charge in a lyrical expression of patriotic feeling.

Lines 198–235: Returning to the mood of the opening, he hopes that the emergency will pass away like the gust of wind that has just 'roared and died away/ In the distant tree', too distant to bend the blades of grass (which suggest ordinary humble people) at his feet. Now, walking home in the dewy twilight, he has a glimpse of the sea and of an expanse of fields and trees. These cheer the mind, giving it 'A livelier impulse and a dance of thought'. In the distance he sees the giant elm-trees around his cottage. The natural scene behind him, and the domestic peace before him, soften his heart.

NOTES AND GLOSSARY:

furze: spiky evergreen shrub with yellow flowers (gorse)
the Book of Life: the Bible
factious: expressive of narrow and extreme party views
or ... or: either ... or
elmy: bordered with elms
the mansion of my friend: Tom Poole's house

The Nightingale (April 1798)

The sub-title 'A conversation poem' has been used by modern critics to describe several of Coleridge's poems. This is the only case in which he uses the term himself, perhaps because this poem more conspicuously addresses his friends and speaks of 'we' and 'our'. It is certainly, after a brief descriptive introduction, a chatty poem, distinguished by its high spirits and sociable air rather than by real poetic power.

Obliquely (that is, by negations and implication rather than direct statement) the opening lines evoke a dark night, in which only the glimmering stream can be detected, beneath the bridge on which Coleridge stands with his friends. The night is still, and darkened by a cloudy sky bringing spring rains. A nightingale sings, and Coleridge quotes Milton's phrase 'Most musical, most melancholy', only to dismiss the idea as an 'idle thought'. In a note Coleridge explains that Milton was not himself guilty of calling the nightingale melancholy; rather he was expressing the feelings of an imagined melancholy character. The idea that nightingales are melancholy is an instance of what we now call 'pathetic fallacy', by which men project their own moods on to nature. In nature, Coleridge protests, 'there is nothing melancholy'. Yet lesser poets echo the conceit, and 'poetical' youths and maidens who know nothing about nature still think of the nightingale's song as a plea for pity.

But Coleridge and his friends know better. The nightingale, in tune with nature, is merry—and his song is rapid only because he is afraid the night will be too short for his love song (43–9).

Lines 49–86 tell an anecdote set in a wild grove, near an uninhabited castle, where nightingales throng the woods so thickly that their eyes may be seen glistening in the night. The playful reference to the 'love-torch' of the glow-worm introduces 'a most gentle Maid' who walks the woods at night as if to meet her lover. Often she has heard the nightingales burst into 'choral minstrelsy' to greet the moon, 'as if some sudden gale had swept at once/ A hundred airy harps' (compare the role of the moon, here, with the 'intellectual Breeze' metaphor in 'The Eolian Harp'). Their song is wanton, like 'tipsy Joy'.

The final verse paragraph is a prolonged 'farewell', in the course of which Coleridge tells his friends, and us, a 'father's tale' about his son Hartley. Once, when the baby had woken sobbing from a nightmare, Coleridge carried him out into the night, where the sight of the moon hushed and cheered him instantly.

NOTES AND GLOSSARY:

strain:	portion of a musical tune
conceit:	conception. 'Conceit' is also a literary term for a witty conception wittily, and sometimes elaborately, expressed. To the extent that Coleridge regards it as a 'figure of speech' to call the nightingale's song melancholy, this literary meaning is a secondary one in this context
poet who:	that is, many a poet who (since his lines have ten syllables each, and the indefinite article would make eleven, Coleridge risks this rather clumsy ellipsis)
Philomela:	the name of a maiden who in Greek mythology was turned into a nightingale
jug jug:	a phrase used by poets from the Elizabethan age down to T. S. Eliot (1888–1965)—in 'The Waste Land' (1922)—to express the sound of the nightingale
something more than Nature:	strictly speaking, this phrase could mean either God or man. The lady could be vowed and dedicated to either, but Coleridge's ambiguity is surely playful in this context and suggests a lover
what time:	when. This usage is especially associated with Milton, one of whose lines is quoted here, in line 13
tipsy:	pleasantly inebriated
that strain again:	probably an allusion to William Shakespeare's famous opening lines in *Twelfth Night*—'If music be

Joy:

the food of love, play on. ... That strain again; it had a dying fall' despite the reference to 'tipsy Joy' in line 86, Joy is a key term in Coleridge's poetry, used to describe the fundamental spirit of life and nature. Because the 'one Life' *is* Joy, it is not a pathetic fallacy (in the argument of the poem) to hear the nightingale's song as joyful

---

Kubla Khan (1797–8)

This poem is usually prefaced by Coleridge's note of 1816 explaining how it came to be written, but not all editions include the brief comment found in one of the manuscripts of the poem:

> This fragment with a good deal more, not recoverable, composed, in a sort of reverie brought on by two grains of opium taken to check a dysentery, at a Farm House between Porlock and Linton [on the North Devon coast], a quarter of a mile from Culbone Church, in the fall of the year, 1797.

Despite this note the poem was probably finished in 1798, and was certainly not written 'instantly' as the longer note claims. Notice that the full title is 'Kubla Khan or, a Vision in a Dream. A Fragment', and that before he began to dream he had been reading 'the following sentence, or words of the same substance, in Purchas's *Pilgrimage*: "Here the Khan Kubla commanded a palace to be built, and a stately garden thereunto. And thus ten miles of fertile ground were inclosed within a wall."' The actual words in Purchas's *Pilgrimage* (1613) are 'In Xamdu did Cublai Can build a stately Palace....'

The poem begins by describing the siting of a 'pleasure-dome' at a point where the sacred river Alph plunges through a gorge into caves and an underground sea. A wall is built to enclose a fertile paradise of gardens, streams and groves.

The second paragraph describes the already existing works of nature, the 'deep romantic chasm' which is both 'savage' and 'holy'—a fitting place for a story in romance. The force of water is described in terms which suggest turmoil, erosion and fertility all at once. The river meanders for five miles before it reaches the caverns and disappears in tumult. This tumult, again in a dream-like way, seems prophetic of war (we do not know whether the ancestral voices are prophesying that Kubla will face a time of war, or that they themselves will—nor does it matter, since conflict is eternal).

Lines 31–6 evoke imagery which is both precise and dream-like, complex and fluid: a still shadow 'floating' on the rapid waves, where sounds of the thrusting fountain and of the measureless caves can both be heard. To complete this scene of paradoxes, the dome itself is both sunny and possessed of caves of ice. Paradox continues in the following lines, which present a 'vision' of music—in which an Abyssinian maid sings of Mount Abora, while playing her dulcimer.

This poem, which calls itself a fragment, and is presented as an interrupted composition which Coleridge could not 'revive' once he had been interrupted (by the real or imaginary 'person from Porlock'), concludes with a stanza about being unable to revive within him the 'symphony and song' of the maid. In other words, Coleridge's strange account of the composition of the poem is also, mysteriously, an account of what happens within the poem. Similarly, Coleridge and Kubla become intertwined. Could he revive the maiden's song, he too would build a pleasure dome—the same ('that dome'), yet not the same, for he would build 'in air' and 'with music'. He would be like Kubla, but his dome would be still more ideal. And with his 'flashing eyes, his floating hair' he would be a true prophet, unlike Kubla who merely hears prophecy. His music would enable all who heard to see what he imagines.

NOTES AND GLOSSARY:

Alph, Abyssinia, Abora: Alph is probably a contraction of Alpheus, a river which is mentioned in classical texts as having prolonged underground sections, and is associated with the Nile (the sacred river). Abyssinia (Ethiopia) is the traditional site of Paradise. Mount Abora does not exist. Its name combines that of the river Abola, a tributary of the Nile, with Mt Amara—a real mountain which is mentioned in two of Coleridge's sources, *Pilgrimage* by Samuel Purchas (1575–1626; editor of several works of religious history and journals of great explorers) and Milton's description of Paradise in *Paradise Lost*, Book 4. These names are discussed extensively in J. L. Lowes, *The Road to Xanadu,* Constable, London, 1927

sinuous rills: small, winding streams

athwart: crossing obliquely

Abyssinian: apart from the oriental and paradisal connotations, the maid is Abyssinian for the pleasing verbal effect of counterpointing 'abyss' with 'mount'

dulcimer: an instrument on which sounds are produced, as in the piano, by hammers striking strings. The word 'dulcet' means sweet and soothing

The Rime of the Ancient Mariner (1797–1816)

The version of this poem now generally read was published in 1816. The poem as published in 1798 was full of deliberately archaic vocabulary. It also lacked the prose glosses in the margin. These should be read carefully. They are not merely a summary: they clarify and comment on the verse tale.

Part 1: The Mariner appears at a wedding party, uninvited, and stops one of the guests. Although annoyed, the Wedding-Guest is so mesmerised by the Mariner's 'glittering eye' that 'he cannot choose but hear'. As the Mariner describes the beginning of his voyage southwards we are still aware of the sounds of the wedding feast, and of the Wedding-Guest's impatience, but the Mariner persists with his strangely urgent tale. A fierce gale has driven the Mariner's ship into the icy regions of Antarctica, which are described with vivid precision. An Albatross appears and is welcomed by the crew. It appears to bring good luck, for the ship finds its way safely through ice and fog as it sails north. By now the Wedding-Guest is alarmed by something in the Mariner's expression. In the dramatic last lines of Part 1 the Mariner confesses to a crime (against nature, against hospitality, and against the crew's belief that the Albatross is 'a Christian soul'): 'With my cross-bow/ I shot the Albatross'.

NOTES AND GLOSSARY:
eftsoons: *(archaic)* soon afterwards
kirk: *(Scottish)* church

Part 2: The ship sails north, still in mist. The sailors are uneasy, sensing that it was unwise to kill the bird which brought them a southerly wind. But as the mists clear they change their tune and associate themselves with his act. They enter the 'silent' Pacific ocean and sail on until they are again at the equator, at which latitude they are becalmed. Lines 111–38 describe this becalming in vivid, memorable terms, stressing the stillness, their thirst, and the 'slimy things . . . upon the slimy sea'. Superstition takes hold of the sailors. Believing that the Mariner has offended one of the spirits of the elements, they make him wear the Albatross about his neck, in place of the crucifix.

NOTES AND GLOSSARY:
averred: swore
uprist: rose up
Ah! well a-day!: an archaic idiom, meaning 'what a woeful time it was!'

Part 3: Time passes. Then, one day, the Mariner sees 'a something' in the distance. To moisten his throat the Mariner bites his arm, drawing blood, and shouts to his companions. A sail is approaching, with neither wind nor current to propel her. At sunset the strange vessel arrives between them and the setting sun: it is a skeleton ship and her only crew are spectres, 'Death' and 'Life-in-Death'. As they arrive the spectres are casting dice. Life-in-Death wins the game, as night falls, and her prize is the soul of the Mariner. All the rest of the crew die that night: 'And every soul, it passed me by/ Like the whizz of my cross-bow!' (The word 'cross' or 'cross-bow' appears in the last or next last line of each part so far).

NOTES AND GLOSSARY:
wist: *(archaic)* knew
unslaked: unsatisfied (that is, dry)
weal: good, good fortune
Heaven's Mother: Mary, mother of Jesus ('Mother of God')
clomb: climbed

Part 4: The Wedding-Guest is now still more alarmed, thinking that he must be listening to a ghost. But the Mariner assures him, 'this body dropped not down'. Yet his experience was worse than death. Lines 232–47 describe the experience of 'Life-in-Death'—alone among slimy and rotting things, unable to avoid the curse he sees in the eyes of his dead companions, unable to die or to pray. If you have observed the particular role of the moon in other poems by Coleridge you will know that the reference to the moon in line 263 foretells a change. The light of the moon beautifies the sky and the sea. More important, in its clear, cool light the Mariner is revived enough to watch the 'water-snakes' and admire their strange beauty. 'A spring of love gushed from my heart, And I blessed them unaware.' The spring of love makes prayer possible, and the Albatross 'fell off and sank/ Like lead into the sea'.

Part 5: Sleep follows prayer, as a heaven-sent gift. The Mariner dreams of dew, and wakes to find it raining. An uncanny storm follows in which, through lightning and rain, the moon and stars still shine. Although no wind is felt, the ship moves on. The dead bodies of his ship-mates rise and 'work the ropes', animated by 'a troop of spirits'. At dawn the bodies emit sweet sounds like a chorus of angels, and the Mariner is cheered up by sounds like those of birds and instruments; even the sails sound like a stream in 'leafy ... June'. The motion of the ship is caused by supernatural agency, the Polar spirit. A sudden spurt causes the Mariner to swoon, and while unconscious he hears two other spirits discuss his crime, and how the Polar spirit 'loved the bird that loved the man/ Who shot him with his bow' (in lines 399–401 the words 'cross', 'bow' and 'Albatross' recur). The other spirit refers to the penance the Mariner has done, and prophesies that he 'penance more will do'.

NOTES AND GLOSSARY:

silly:	blessed (an archaic meaning, from the German *selig*)
corses:	corpses
jargoning:	twittering of birds, but related to 'jargon' meaning unfamiliar or unintelligible speech
swound:	swoon, fainting fit

Part 6: The voices continue their debate. The second voice explains that the ocean is so still because the moon, its master, is in gracious mood; and that the ship moves at such speed because it is propelled by a vacuum effect (the marginal gloss further emphasises the supernatural speed of the vessel). The Mariner awakes to find himself sailing in fair weather, but still observed by the crew of 'deadmen'. He turns away from the curse in their eyes and soon sees land approaching (lines 465–8 repeat the images of lines 21–4 in reverse order, except that the return is made by moonlight). As he enters harbour he turns his eyes 'upon the deck' and sees a seraph standing by each fallen corpse. A rowing-boat approaches, bringing the Pilot and his boy, and a Hermit. The sound of the Hermit's voice brings hope to the Mariner: 'He'll shrieve my soul, he'll wash away/ The Albatross's blood'.

NOTES AND GLOSSARY:

shrieve:	archaic form of 'shrive', itself an archaic word meaning to hear a penitent's confession, assign penance, and absolve from sin (part of the duties of a Roman Catholic priest)

Part 7: The Mariner continues to think of the Hermit, who lives alone with nature. As the pilot's boat approaches, the Mariner hears them discussing the strange appearance of the ship and its now vanished seraph-lights. A thunderous sound is heard, and the ship sinks; the stunned Mariner is pulled aboard the Pilot's boat. When he tries to speak his rescuers react strangely—the Pilot faints, his boy goes crazy, and the Hermit begins to pray: the Mariner has to row the boat himself. Ashore, he begins his confession, and this relieves his agony. But the penance of the Mariner cannot end. He goes 'like night, from land to land' and has 'strange power of speech'; and wherever he goes he recognises the kind of man who needs to hear his tale. One such man is the Wedding-Guest, and the poem ends by making him the central figure. The Mariner's last words are a message to him, concerning the

loneliness of the soul without God, the necessity of prayer, and the uselessness of prayer without love. The Mariner is gone. Only the Wedding-Guest remains, 'stunned' and 'forlorn': 'A sadder and a wiser man,/ He rose the morrow morn.'

NOTES AND GLOSSARY:

ivy-tod: clump or mass of ivy

Christabel (1800–1)

As 'Christable' is a narrative poem, the fact that it is unfinished is rather frustrating. Yet for many readers it is one of Coleridge's most fascinating productions. Although the narrative is fragmentary, the imagined world, the tone and the atmosphere are fully achieved—and it is for the poet's vision, rather than for the tale, that we read poetry.
Part 1, lines 1–70: The scene is a castle, at midnight, marked not only by owls but more uncannily by a crowing cock, and by the Baron's 'mastiff bitch' which 'answers' the clock in 'short howls'. It is a chill April night, lit by a small, dull moon. Sir Leonine's daughter, Christabel, is in the wood beyond the castle gate, to pray for her 'betrothed knight' (like the maid in 'The Nightingale' she is a child of nature). Praying beneath an oak she is startled by a moan. This comes not from the wind (for lines 45–52 capture the stillness in precise images) but from 'a damsel bright', beautiful and richly clad in white.
Lines 71–189: To explain her presence, Geraldine claims that she has been kidnapped by warriors, brought far on horseback, and for some unknown reason left beneath the oak. Christabel offers the hospitality of her father's house, and they enter the sleeping castle. As they pass the mastiff bitch she moans ominously in her sleep. The embers of the fire in the hall also react with 'a fit of flame' as the women pass silently to Christabel's bedroom.
Lines 190–225: To revive her guest, Christabel offers a glass of healing cordial. This was made by her mother, who died in childbirth, saying that she would, though dead, hear Christabel's wedding-bells. Geraldine reacts strangely, staring as if at the ghost of Christabel's mother, and warning her that 'this hour is mine'. Christabel responds sympathetically to this outburst and soothes Geraldine, who drinks the cordial. As she revives her eyes become bright and she is seen in her full beauty.
Lines 226–78. Geraldine speaks courteously, blessing Christabel and telling her to prepare for bed. But Christabel watches Geraldine carefully, and as her visitor undresses sees something alarming: 'Behold! her bosom and half her side—/ A sight to dream of, not to tell', at which the narrator exclaims, 'O shield her! shield sweet Christabel'. In revising the poem Coleridge inexplicably removed a line explaining that

Geraldine's body appears old and withered 'and foul of hue', but he left the reference (in line 270) to 'this mark of my shame'. Geraldine takes Christabel in her arms and warns her that the touch of her breast will cast a spell over the girl, sealing her lips. All she will be able to say is that she found 'a bright lady' and rescued her.

Lines 279–331: The Conclusion to Part 1 reverts to the oak tree and the lovely sight of Christabel at her prayers, contrasting her beauty and tranquillity then with her anxiety now; but 'the worker of these harms' seems to sleep peacefully. The 'hour' of Geraldine's power (her sorcery?) has passed. While it lasted even the owls were silent; now they call again. Christabel, too, relaxes. Though crying a little, she also smiles, as though her mother's guardian spirit were near.

NOTES AND GLOSSARY:

mastiff:	a large, strong dog. Mastiffs are frequently found in romances or horror stories because of their frightening appearance
up this way:	the setting of the poem is the Lake District of northwest England
mistletoe:	a parasitic plant with white berries, mentioned in various legends and myths, supposedly a sacred plant to the Druids (the ancient Celtic priesthood), and associated with young lovers at Christmas parties
I wis:	I know
scritch:	screech
But through:	the order is transposed here. 'But through her brain so many thoughts of weal [good] and woe [ill] moved to and fro that . . .'
thou warrest:	you war (struggle)
tairn:	tarn, a mountain lake or pond

Part 2, lines 332–92: It is morning, marked as always in Sir Leonine's castle by the funereal tolling of a bell in memory of his wife. The sounds re-echo in the rocks of the Langdale valley, and on a still morning are followed by the sound of more distant and more cheerful bells. Geraldine wakes, shakes off 'her dread' (one of several signs that she is more suffering than evil), and wakesn Christabel—who is still perplexed, as by a dream, but is struck by Geraldine's gentleness and beauty.

Lines 394–446: Together they go to meet the Baron, who warmly welcomes his guest. It appears that he and Geraldine's father—Lord Roland de Vaux of Tryermaine (whose melodious name he murmurs to himself)—were firm friends in youth. Their friendship had been spoiled by 'whispering tongues' and turned to enmity, but neither found as good a friend again, or could wholly forget the other. Sir Leonine forgets his age as he remembers the youthful Lord Roland, and vows to find and punish those who have harmed his friend's daughter, whom he embraces fondly.

Lines 447–518: Watching this embrace, which is prolonged by Geraldine, Christabel is overcome by fear and sees again the dreadful sight of the previous night. In her shock she 'hisses' so sharply that the knight is startled and looks round—but Christabel is smiling again under Geraldine's spell. She cannot tell what is wrong, when her father asks, and Geraldine—appearing to be very tactful—offers to leave at once. Sir Leonine will not hear of it. He decides to send the bard Bracy to Lord Roland's home on the Scottish border with a message that his daughter is safe and that his old friend longs to see him.

Lines 519–63: Bracy, however, asks for a delay. He has had a dream, or a vision, of evil threatening the nearby wood. Bard Bracy's dream is a symbolic account of the danger Christabel is in, though neither of the women is mentioned. In his dream a dove (Christabel) was attacked by 'a bright green snake/ Coiled around its wings and neck'. The snake (Geraldine) was 'couched' with the dove in the same vaguely erotic, yet threatening way as that in which Geraldine was sharing Christabel's couch. The dream came at midnight, but is still 'upon my eye'.

Lines 564–620: The Baron misinterprets the dream. To him the dove is Geraldine and the snake represents her enemies, whom he promises to crush. He kisses Geraldine, who glances at Christabel with eyes shrunken and dull like a serpent's. Again Christabel shudders 'with a hissing sound' and while Geraldine turns her 'large bright eyes divine' on the father, the daughter can only stare at them. Under Geraldine's influence Christabel's eyes imitate 'that look of dull and treacherous hate', as far as is possible, that is, with 'eyes so innocent and blue'. Recovering from her trance, she begs her father to send 'this woman away', but as she is still under the spell she can give no reason.

Lines 621–55: Sir Leonine, however, is under the spell of Geraldine's beauty. He forgets his love for his daughter and feels only rage that she should dishonour him by such rudeness. Abruptly he orders Bracy to depart. Ignoring his daughter, Sir Leonine leaves with Geraldine.

Lines 656–77: The Conclusion to Part 2 appears to have nothing to do with the story. In fact the little child, 'a limber elf', referred to here is no longer Christabel but Coleridge's own child Hartley. The lines are (like those at the end of 'The Nightingale') 'a father's tale'. They can be read as an excuse for Sir Leonine, suggesting that his anger is a result of excess of love, and that he is dallying with 'wrong that does no harm'. But in this strange ending to the fragment we can see Coleridge turning away from his romantic fiction toward his own domestic situation in 1801. This matter is discussed in Part 3 of these notes.

NOTES AND GLOSSARY:

sacristan: an archaic term for 'sexton' (line 353), a church officer

five and forty beads must tell: a reference to 'counting' prayer-beads, each bead standing for a particular payer. Coleridge's medieval poems use such references to Roman Catholic practices for atmospheric effect. The appeal to 'Jesu, Maria' in line 54 is another example

Bratha Head to Wyndermere: place-names in the Lake District (Brathay and Lake Windermere)

Langdale Pike ... Dungeon-Ghyll: a mountain and a ravine in Great Langdale (spots loved by Coleridge and the Wordsworths)

Borodale: another nearby valley (Borrowdale)

vests ... breasts: the line implies that Christabel is confused by the appearance of 'heaving breasts' where, the previous night, Geraldine's breasts were withered

through: passing between

presence room: the room where the Baron receives guests into his presence

espies: detects, notices

beseem: suit, be appropriate to

waxed: grew

I ween: (in context) in my opinion

tourney-court: field for armed contests between individual knights

bosom old ... bosom cold: these lines make explicit the implied content of lines 252–3 and explain Christabel's returning warmth in lines 324–5

bard: poet or minstrel (in a sense Bracy is Coleridge's poetic representative in this poem, and the person most likely to intuit the real nature of Geraldine)

solemn vest: sober clothing

'And when...': Sir Leonine is imagining Bracy's journey

heaves ... swelling: this part of the dream refers to the courting display of doves and snakes, and has further erotic significance

strong arms: refers to 'thy sire and I'—not the 'beauteous dove'

resigned to: controlled by

limber: lithe, nimble

elf: literally a supernatural or magical being, but here it connotes smallness and (as often in colloquial English) refers to a child

Dejection: an Ode (April 1802)

The relation between the two 'dejection' poems is controversial. Most critics assume that 'Dejection: an Ode' is a revision of 'A Letter to Sara Hutchinson'. The arguments against this view are discussed in Part 3. The ode will be summarised first, partly because the letter actually includes the ode (though the sections are rearranged), and is more easily discussed as a variation on the shorter poem.

In the first of the eight strophes of the ode, the poet depicts his favourite images of wind and moon. The state of the moon (a real moon, on which Dorothy Wordsworth also commented) reminds him of an ancient ballad in which stormy weather is foretold from such a phenomenon. As yet his Aeolian harp is only sobbing dully: the sound irritates him and appears to express his own dull feelings. The sobbing lute and the phantom radiance of the moon combine the images now familiar to us from the conversation poems. But here he is not soothed by them: he longs for the promised storm to come, so that he may feel awed and elevated, startled into similar agitation.

The second strophe specifies his unimpassioned mood in terms of void and dreariness. Though 'wooed' by the thrush to contemplate the evening sky more cheerfully, he has gazed blankly on the beautiful appearances of sky and clouds and stars. They only increase his despair: 'I see, not feel, how beautiful they are'.

The third section reflects on this state of mind. If his own 'genial spirits' fail, what can mere appearances do to cheer him? He could watch for ever, but the outer light will not help unless he also has within himself 'passion and life'. The same thought is presented more intensely and more philosophically in the fourth section, where he refutes the idea that the mind can be elevated by outward things. Nature 'lives' only because man bestows beauty, life and meaning upon it. The transforming light of the moon is only an image for the beautifying light that the 'soul' sheds on what it loves. (We feel that moonlight is beautiful only if we are spiritual enough to see the moonlight's likeness to spirit.)

For the activity of the creative soul Coleridge uses the terms 'light', 'luminous mist' and 'music', all suggesting its 'beauty-making power'. But in the fifth strophe he chooses one term—Joy. In the Romantic period Joy was used to denote a state of being in which there is such internal harmony of spirit that it overflows from the pure soul to beautify the world around. In a state of joy we are 'wedded' to nature (line 68), and the 'dowry' of this wedding is 'a new Earth and a new Heaven'. Whatever charms us—all colours or melodies, appealing to eye or ear (line 73)—is a reflection of our own joy.

In the sixth strophe Coleridge looks back on his life, seeing the waning of this joy. In the past his inner joy made him able to 'dally' with distress.

He was sustained by hope, and felt himself to be creative. Now (line 81) he wonders whether he was in fact sustained by the inner strength of others, rather than his own, for now he has no inner resources to meet his afflictions. In lines 87–93 he appears to regret his investigative analytical pursuits: perhaps the scientific detachment of 'abstruse research' has so infected his whole being that he is now incapable of spontaneous joy.

The seventh strophe, however, brings a change of mood. Coleridge shakes off his 'viperous' thoughts. The lute has ceased to moan. The wind is raving, and the scream of the lute makes Coleridge think of the mountain landscape all around—which is a 'fitter' instrument for such a wind. From the passive, suffering lute Coleridge turns his attention to the wind—which he likens to an actor or a poet, expert in tragic art. In the wind he hears a tale of warriors in defeat; and then a more tender song of a lost and frightened child.

From thoughts of the wider world, its tragedies, and the creative powers at work in it, Coleridge returns to addressing the 'Lady' of strophes 2, 4 and 5. Now he is no longer complaining of his own want of joy. The end of the poem is a prayer that she might be watched over by the bright stars; and that she—unlike the poet—may be visited by healing sleep, and attuned to joy.

NOTES AND GLOSSARY:

yestreen: last evening

Sir Patrick Spence: one of the best-known ballads in Bishop Percy's *Reliques of Ancient English Poetry* (1765)

draft: draught, current of air

wonted: customary

O Lady!: the lady is Sara Hutchinson. Coleridge addresses Sara because he needs her understanding. The concluding prayer of the poem is a gift to her, as the woman he loves most deeply. But the argument of the poem is really addressed to Wordsworth. The first published version of the poem (in *The Morning Post*, 4 October 1802) has 'O Edmund'. A version transcribed in a letter to Southey, 19 July 1802, is explicitly addressed to Wordsworth

give away their motion: that is, they make the stars appear to move

genial: in Coleridge's day the primary meaning of the word was 'generative', 'connected with creative genius'. Nowadays the word means 'jovial' or 'sociable'. The 'generative' meaning is associated also with wedded love, so the phrase is linked with (a) Coleridge's marital unhappiness, (b) the 'wedding' imagery of lines 49 and 68

forms:	shapes or 'things'. Philosophically, 'outward forms' implies material entities as opposed to the realm of eternal ideas
fountains:	a key image in many poems, associated with 'springs' of creativity

we receive but what we give: this part of the poem is most clearly related to Wordsworth's faith in the interaction of nature and the mind and what 'they with *blended might* accomplish' (Wordsworth). Coleridge is questioning one of Wordsworth's most characteristic beliefs

wedding-garment ... shroud: one of the basic themes of Romanticism was that materialist philosophy changed the living world into a world of death. Coleridge is not identifying himself with materialist thought, but he is lamenting that if the observer is not full of joy the world is, subjectively, dead to him

Joy: the reiteration of joy in this passage is similar to that in a famous German Romantic poem—Friedrich Schiller's 'Ode to Joy'. Schiller's text is sung by the chorus in Beethoven's Ninth Symphony with its triumphant repetition of *'Freude ... Freude'* ('Joy ... Joy')

We in ourselves rejoice!: Wordsworth testifies in his poetry that if one looks into the 'life of things' one finds that joy is the basis of all life. Coleridge retorts here that the joy we find in nature is really in ourselves

There was a time ...: an allusion to the first line of Wordsworth's 'Ode: Intimations of Immortality'—'There was a time when meadow, grove, and stream/ ... To me did seem/ Apparelled in celestial light'

Otway's self: Thomas Otway (1652–85), a dramatic poet. Line 210 of the verse letter refers more pertinently to 'William's self' as the author of the 'tender lay'. But Otway, who died a tragic early death, was for Coleridge one of those whose lives embody the fatality of being a poet

---

Letter to Sara Hutchinson (1802)

The letter begins with a paragraph almost identical to the first strophe of the ode, except that Sara is addressed in line 15. The account of dread is the same, except that Coleridge appeals to Sara as one who knows what he suffers. The singing thrush (24–9) is more specifically located in a larch tree coming into leaf. By placing the words 'vainly wooed' (which refer to the thrush's song) next to 'O dearest Sara', Coleridge delicately alludes to his love for her. The moon of lines 39–40 is also made more personal: his image of the moon becalmed in its blue lake is now associated with 'dear William's sky canoe' (a reference to Wordsworth's poem 'Peter Bell').

The opening lines of the third paragraph correspond to lines 39–46 of the ode, but lines 52–184 appear in the letter alone. The 'green light' image now introduces the thought that Sara may be watching the same light. Even this thought moves him only feebly, although he remembers that as a schoolboy he was moved to ecstatic yearnings by such sights and reflections. Yet in lines 74–98 it appears that his despair at non-feeling was rash, for the reflection has affected him: he imagines Sara in two favourite places and he is, after all, moved by the thought. Imagining her, he sees in her eyes a 'prayer' meant for him: his response is to bless her.

Lines 99–110 recall an evening with Mary and Sara, when he enjoyed the innocent affection of both sisters. Such remembrances of joy revive him; but he wonders why he was unable to recall such memories a short time before. Line 115 refers to having written a complaining letter to Sara. Perhaps over-dramatically, he blames Sara's present sickness (116–29) on his painful, bruising letter. The letter seems to have concerned the feelings between them (or the lack of them on her part) for in lines 130–78 he makes an attempt to persuade her that he will not claim more than she can give. Her well-being and tranquillity are all he desires, and he will be content to think of William, Mary, Dorothy and Sara living together in happiness. He would rather not see their happiness, however, as temporary visits only lead to the pain of parting. The imagery of lines 160–8 makes plain the strength of Coleridge's feeling that he is an outsider, unable to share fully in their joy: he feels himself to be 'A wither'd branch upon a blossoming Tree'. He will be content to share her delights at a distance—but he confesses that he cannot bear to be unable to comfort her when she is in need.

Lines 184–224 return to the sound of the lute and the now raving wind (as in 94–133 of the ode). The prayer that his friend may enjoy gentle and healing sleep is followed in this poem by another personal lament over his own lack of buoyancy.

The passage 'there was a time . . .' now appears, at a later point in the letter than in the ode, and perhaps with increased effect—since the loss of imaginative power is felt here as an additional burden to be borne. And a reference to Coleridge's own domestic discord adds to the sense of grievance (243–8).

Lines 249–64 contrast the Wordsworths' family of love with his own 'coarse' domestic life. His 'abstruse research' appears, in this context, to have been a way of trying to distract himself from this sense of grievance, though this claim is not entirely convincing in the light of Coleridge's biography.

Even the joy he finds in his own children reminds him of how much he has lost; at times he feels resentment at being burdened by them, and cramped in his intellectual flights (line 280). Although he cannot claim to find no solace in the beauty of the Lake District, its scenes are not what they once were.

The letter ends with passages equivalent to strophes 4 and 5 of the ode, and a modified version of its final lines.

NOTES AND GLOSSARY:

leafits: young 'needles' of the larch tree
Hearts of finer mould: finer hearts than mine
weather-fended wood: sheltered
sod-built Seat of Camomile: a seat built of sods of grassy earth, in which is growing the aromatic plant camomile
O Sister: Sara's sister was about to become Wordsworth's wife, and of course Dorothy's sister-in-law. All of them looked on Coleridge as a brother
Mary: Mary Hutchinson and William Wordsworth married on 4 October 1802, the day Coleridge published an early version of the Ode
I too will crown me with a Coronal: an allusion to Wordsworth's 'Immortality Ode', line 40 ('My head hath its coronal'). The following lines contrast his own indolence with Wordsworth's productivity
Of Yore: in the past

The Pains of Sleep (1803)

This poem is a vivid portrayal of psychological unease, a very personal confession. Apart from its intrinsic interest it adds depth to the references to 'sleep' in such poems as 'The Ancient Mariner', 'Christabel' and the 'Dejection' poems.

The first paragraph evokes calm preparation for sleep. It stresses quietness and composure, spiritual resignation and blessedness. The poet seems to think that formal prayer is unnecessary: instead he goes through a private ritual of 'composing' his spirit to love. The rhyme in 'compose' and 'close' gives a sense of physical self-composure. The rhymes 'exprest', 'imprest', 'blest', with their sibilants, evoke the sleeper's quiet breathing. Notice how 's' sounds recur, voiced and unvoiced, in all thirteen lines: limb*s*, u*s*e, lip*s*, knee*s*, *s*ilently, degree*s*, . . . wi*sh* conceived, . . . *s*en*s*e, *s*oul impre*st*, and so on.

In the second paragraph a different experience is recorded. Sleep is disturbed by nightmare and dread. He is tortured by thoughts of being wronged, of desiring revenge, and of guilt. The line 'Desire with loathing strangely mixed' is a precise definition of existential dread. Here the violence of the emotional turmoil is evoked partly by the violent terms employed (anguish, fiendish, trampling, hateful, maddening) and partly by the powerful stresses on such terms as aloud, anguish, agony, suffered, did, guilt and woe. Vigorous stresses are combined with clusters of assonance and alliteration throughout: *ang*uish/ *agon*y; *th*ough*t*/ *tort*ured; fant*a*stic/ m*a*ddening; *l*urid/ *l*ight; *b*affled/ *b*urning.

By the third such night, he had come to fear sleep as 'distemper's worst calamity'. But his scream on waking from a nightmare brings calming tears. At the end of the poem he appears to achieve a kind of peace, but only by convincing himself that he does not deserve such griefs, which are more appropriate to 'natures deepliest stained with sin'. Rather smugly he describes himself as deserving better: 'To be beloved is all I need/ And whom I love, I love indeed'. The tone is so self-congratulatory, in distinguishing himself from the wicked, that we detect in the closing lines some explanation of the preceding restlessness. Coleridge shows himself demanding love unconditionally, but bestowing it conditionally or selectively. This is combined with a self-righteous attitude toward men who are really wicked and who deserve to suffer.

There are in fact two contrary interpretations of the poem. Like the conversation poems (and this poem is a conversation between his waking self and his sleeping self) this poem has a circular structure. It begins and ends with an apparent sense of calm. In our interpretation we can either take the asserted calmness at its face value, or we can see it as implying self-deception. The complacent conclusion (he is better than other men, so he should not suffer) is parallel to the smug opening (because he is superior to other men he need not pray 'on bended knees'). The reason for believing that Coleridge is dramatising a state of self-deception, rather than actually deceiving himself, is that lines 45–8, which are clearly about other men, duplicate the substance of 23–6, which are equally clearly about himself.

You may not be convinced by this interpretation. Is it a poem *about* self-deception? Or is it merely a self-deceiving poem?

To William Wordsworth (1807)

The occasion of this poem was a reading by Wordsworth of his long philosophical poem *The Prelude*, which deals in fourteen books with the growth of the poet's own mind, as a prelude to an even longer project (never completed) which Coleridge had proposed to him. Lines 1–47 are a succinct account of Wordsworth's theme. They describe how *The Prelude* tackles the revolutionary subject of how the 'human spirit' is built up, the poet's account of his childhood amid natural scenery, his life in revolutionary France and his disillusion, and the concluding themes of this 'song divine'—Duty, Action and Joy.

In lines 48–75 Coleridge describes his dual response: on the one hand his admiration for Wordsworth's achievement (Wordsworth is one of the 'truly great', an immortal poet); and on the other, his painful sense of his own relative failure to fulfil his promise. Characteristically he criticises himself (76–82) for this absorption with his own problems. He hopes that Wordsworth will remember not his lament but the exalted 'communion' that took place between them after the recitation.

Lines 92–112 revert to describing the impression made by Wordsworth's poem. His soul 'lay passive', as if sailing, enjoying the phosphorescent foam in the wake of Wordsworth's thoughts and his own. Sometimes he felt like the sea itself, responsive to the moon of Wordsworth's poetry. The reading left him in a mingled state of thought, aspiration and resolve, 'and when I rose, I found myself in prayer'. One of the ways in which Coleridge pays tribute to Wordsworth in this poem is by employing frequent verbal allusions both to Wordsworth's own poetry and to that of his great predecessor, Milton.

Work without Hope (1825)

In this poem, one of the most moving of his later works, Coleridge contrasts the busy stir of nature with his own 'unbusy' self. Even the winter is enlivened by dreams of spring. Although he knows of the 'amaranth' (an imaginary unfading flower) and of streams of nectar (the drink of the gods), these are not for him. That is, he cannot attain the higher slopes of poetic achievement. His brow is 'wreathless', without the victor's garland. The concluding couplet finely expresses his lack of hope. With nothing to hope for, one cannot hope; and to work without hope is like trying to draw nectar 'in a sieve'.

Epitaph (1833)

An epitaph is a form of words intended to be inscribed on a gravestone. In this famous epitaph for himself Coleridge speaks as one who once 'seemed' to be a poet. He asks not for praise, but for a gentle thought and a prayer. He sees himself as having experienced—like his own Ancient Mariner—death-in-life, but through prayer and through faith in Christ he hopes to find 'life in death'.

Part 3
Commentary

The literary background

Romanticism

Literary history classifies Coleridge as one of the great Romantic poets—the others being Blake, Wordsworth, Byron, Shelley and Keats. Romanticism is not merely a period classification. The lifetimes of these poets span the period between 1757, when Blake was born, and 1850, when Wordsworth died. Their really productive period runs from 1789, when Blake printed his *Songs of Innocence*, to 1824, the year of Byron's death and of the last cantos of his *Don Juan*. Throughout this period many poets and novelists were active whom no one would call Romantic. The phenomenon known as Romanticism is dated differently in each country—England, Germany, Italy, France, Poland, Russia, Spain and America experienced Romanticism at different times and in various forms, from the late eighteenth century to the end of the nineteenth.

A common fallacy defines Romanticism as the antithesis to Realism. This has arisen because the term 'Romantic' is originally the adjectival form of Romance—a literary genre, mainly medieval, which usually tells a story set in a purely fictional, fantasy world, in which supernatural events are common, and in which moral values are clearer and simpler than in the real world. Those who use the term 'Romantic' in this sense tend to emphasise the idealism of the Romantic poets, their alleged fondness for the past (either a remote 'golden age' or the mysterous medieval world), their moods of melancholy or nostalgia, and so forth. Of course, all the features are to be found in Romanticism, just as they are in the literature of many ages. Romanticism, however, should not be confused with escapism.

It is true that the Romantics were interested in creating something other than the 'everyday world'. They took a critical, sometimes revolutionary attitude toward contemporary life. But they were engaged in the serious task of projecting in their poems the potential of human life. What they opposed to the existing everyday world was not a private fantasy world but a record of their own finest experiences and a vision of what life, ideally, can be.

Sometimes the term 'Romanticism' is opposed to 'Classicism'. This, too, is misleading. Many Romantic works are 'classics' of literature: many Classical texts are Romantic in inception—and the works of Homer and Shakespeare, one might say, are the classic Romantic texts. It is, however, correct to observe a distinction between neo-Classical writing—in which the writer is governed by social decorum and the established norms of literature—and the more individual, experimental, expressive tendency of the Romantic writer.

One of the primary marks of a Romantic artist is an interest in nature. To poets in the Romantic period (in England especially), eighteenth-century thought had led to an artificial distinction between man and nature—between the thinking mind and the dead material world which was the object of its thought. To the Romantics this stress on analytical thought was reductive: they were interested in the vitality of the 'whole man', one of whose essential capacities is that of enjoying a creative relationship with the natural world. The rationalist view was, to them, unrealistic: in separating man from nature it failed to recognise whole areas of *human* nature. When, says Coleridge, a man's aim is commercial or materialist, he exploits the world as a realm of objects. But when his aim is 'the nurture and evolution of humanity', he seeks what is 'common to the world and to man'. Man cannot understand either himself or nature until he learns 'to comprehend nature in himself'.

Another Romantic characteristic is to stress, and take delight in, man's imaginative power. The fact that human beings are capable of visionary experience as well as sight, intuition as well as deduction, inventiveness as well as imitation, is to be rejoiced in: he is not merely a slave of his material perceptions.

The Romantic believes, too, that the way to realise the best potential in human nature is not through repression of whatever is individual, eccentric, and unconventional, but through liberation of human energies. The purpose of life, says Coleridge, is to produce 'the highest and most comprehensive individuality' *(Theory of Life)*, so 'every state of life which is not progressive is dead or retrograde' *(The Friend)*. Energy is essentially innocent and creative: man, as a natural being, is also a developing being, capable of creating new forms of order and beauty. The Romantic's admiration of nature is part of his love of the growing and the organic: a love of nature and a faith in political progress are aspects of the same faith—essentially a commitment to flux rather than stasis. The characteristic Romantic poem shows its hero, often the poet, in the process of discovering something about the world or himself, or in the process of becoming.

A stress upon the importance of the individual is something the Romantics share with Existentialist philosophy. Only individuals (that is, those who stand upon their own authority, rather than relying upon collective values) can be fully authentic. Knowing, believing, and acting, are individual matters, or they have no meaning. Coleridge observes very characteristically, in *The Friend*, that 'the first step to knowledge, or rather the previous condition of all insight into truth, is to dare to commune with our very and permanent self'. If we do not know ourselves, we can know nothing. But this belief in the individual is combined with a faith in the unity of humanity. The test of individual belief is its 'universal validity', Coleridge says, also in *The Friend*, for 'there is one heart for the whole mighty mass of Humanity'.

Romantic poets also tend to share a sense of the special role of poets. They see their task as being to share with humanity a unique but humanly central vision, and they speak of themselves as teachers, or physicians, or prophets. But their teaching is not usually through bald statement. Most Romantic poems attempt to provide not merely a message but an experience. Their work is intended to educate the reader by making him feel, think or see, in ways that are beyond his normal experience. One of the functions of the poet is 'so to represent familiar objects as to awaken the minds of others to a like freshness of sensation concerning them'. Another is to remind us of truths, for 'truths are too often considered as so true that they lose all the powers of truth, and lie bed-ridden in the dormitory of the soul...' *(The Friend)*.

Romantic poetry is recognisably imaginative, symbolic and myth-ological, in literary terms. We see in the Romantics, too, a particular fondness for intensity, diversity, and the ever-changing. But these factors are deployed in the poetry with two over-riding intentions: to reconnect man with the spiritual resources of his own nature, and to overcome the division between man and organic nature.

Eighteenth-century poetry

There is some truth in the view that Romanticism was a reaction against the prevailing philosophy and sensibility of the eighteenth century, which is marked by the prevalence, in literature and thought, of wit, reason, order and restraint. The most characteristic literature of the eighteenth century is polished, commonsensical, socially assured, and refined in tone and style: it rarely embodies significant emotion, or originality of thought or action. If the key term in the Romantic era was 'Imagination', that of the preceding age was 'Taste'.

Yet Coleridge and his contemporaries were strongly influenced by some eighteenth-century ideas and literary models. Their perception of landscape, for instance, and of man's place in it, is not entirely new. Wild, 'Romantic' landscapes had begun to appear in eighteenth-century verse. It was in 1757 that Edmund Burke published his *Enquiry into the Origin of our Ideas of the Sublime and the Beautiful*. The Romantic poets would refine his psychology, but he too felt the power of vast or terrifying natural scenes to produce 'the strongest emotions which the mind is capable of feeling'. The Romantics were to some extent helped by their predecessors in the study of how sublime sights in nature can elevate, expand and purify the mind and feelings of the beholder. Even in childhood, Coleridge says, 'my mind had been habituated to the vast, and I never regarded my senses in any way as the criteria of my belief' (letter to Poole, 16 October 1797). It is the desire 'to behold and know something *great*—something one and indivisible' that makes 'rocks or waterfalls, mountains or caverns give me the sense of sublimity or majesty'. Looked at in that spirit, 'all things counterfeit infinity' (letter to Thelwall, 14 October 1797).

In poetry and the visual arts, sublime scenery was fashionable in the late eighteenth century. Some of the poets of that period—those Coleridge admired—had also begun to enquire into man's relationship to nature in something of a Romantic spirit. The Reverend William Lisle Bowles (1762–1850) published a book of *Fourteen Sonnets* in 1789 which inspired Coleridge to write a sonnet in praise of him. What Coleridge admired in such poems as 'The River Itchin' (which he imitated in 'The River Otter') was Bowles's use of convincing natural imagery, his tenderness, and his occasional sublimity. Coleridge's imitation, however, far surpasses the original.

Similarly, Coleridge imitates and extends the work of William Cowper (1731–1800), who wrote in meditative blank verse about natural scenes and domestic feelings. His poetry is more detached and more moralising than that of Wordsworth or Coleridge, yet 'Frost at Midnight' borrows a good deal of imagery and observation from a similar fireside scene in Cowper's long poem *The Task* (1784).

Coleridge is similarly indebted to James Beattie (1735–1803), whose poem *The Minstrel* (1774) traces the education by nature of a shepherd's poetical powers; and to Mark Akenside (1721–70) whose *Pleasures of the Imagination* (1744) is a remarkable forerunner of Wordsworth's work. Akenside fails to combine poetry and thought with the ease and power of the Romantics, but he has a similar aim, which is to produce a moral effect by exposing the reader to emotively engaging natural scenes.

Although their own imaginative powers were much superior, Wordsworth and Coleridge admired what was original in these pioneers. Of course, they were also aware of their deficiences. There is an illuminating criticism of Bowles in Coleridge's letter to Southey of 10 September 1802. Bowles's faults are his 'moralising' and his 'loose mixture' of natural images and moral analogies. Rather, he says, 'a poet's heart and intellect should be *combined*, intimately combined and unified with the great appearances of nature'.

Coleridge as poet and critic

It is in achieving this unity that Coleridge made his first great contribution to Romantic poetry—fitfully in his early nature poems, and superlatively in the conversation poems. And although it is not as 'nature poetry' that we value the visionary poems, they too benefit from what became a habit of his soul.

There is surprisingly little difference between the symbols used in his most dramatic and his most intimate poems. One of Coleridge's remarks about symbolism applies to all his poetry:

> In looking at objects of Nature while I am thinking, as at yonder moon dim-glimmering through the dewy window-pane, I seem rather to be seeking, as it were *asking* for, a symbolical language for something within me that already and for ever exists, than observing anything new. Even when that latter is the case, yet still I have always an obscure feeling as if that new phenomenon were the dim awakening of a forgotten or hidden truth of my inner nature. *(Anima Poetae)*

Notice how 'dim-glimmering' that particular image is. Nature, in Coleridge's poetry, is somehow minutely naturalistic, highly subjective, and yet plainly symbolic at the same time. That is, we see nature projected with sensuous clarity. We also see that the choice of objects, and the way they are used in Coleridge's meditation, makes them revelatory of his own states of feeling. And yet these same images, often moonlit or starlit, are of universal rather than private significance. If this world of images is frequently shadowy—except in 'The Ancient Mariner' which belongs to the spirit-realm—the reason is that Coleridge was deeply Platonic in his thought. For him, the material world *is* shadowy, in the philosophic sense that 'appearances' are the shadows, or reflections of 'ideas' projected on the flux of time. The material world, that is, merely reflects the *real* world of Ideas. To use his own words, in the *Philosophical Lectures:* 'Plato ... conceived that the phenomenon [what is seen] ... is but a language by which the invisible ... communicates its existence to our finite beings'.

Perhaps the best way to summarise what Coleridge achieved in his very best poems is to quote his famous definition, in *Biographia Literaria*, Chapter 14, of the ideal poet:

> The poet, described in *ideal* perfection, brings the whole soul of man into activity, with the subordination of its faculties to each other, according to their relative worth and dignity.

The 'whole soul of man' comprises, for Coleridge, reason, faith, will, understanding and feeling. The synthesis is brought about by Imagination:

This power ... reveals itself in the balance or reconciliation of opposite or discordant qualities; of sameness, with difference; of the general, with the concrete; the idea, with the image; the individual, with the representative; the sense of novelty and freshness, with old and familiar objects; a more than usual state of emotion, with more than usual order; judgement ever awake and steady self-possession, with enthusiasm and feeling profound or vehement; and while it blends and harmonises the natural and the artificial, still subordinates art to nature....*

In a lecture of 1818 Coleridge made another useful generalisation about poetry, using Milton's idea that poetry should be 'simple, sensuous and passionate':

It is essential to poetry that it be simple, and appeal to the elements and primary laws of our nature; that it be sensuous, and by its imagery elicit truth at a flash; that it be impassioned, and be able to move our feelings and awaken our affections.

Exquisite language and fine metre do not make good poetry, for 'it is not poetry, if it make no appeal to our passions or our imagination'.

Coleridge is of the highest originality as a critic. He provided some of the most probing accounts of poetic imagination, and exhibited a model of precise critical analysis of texts. Central to his theory is the term 'Imagination'. 'The *Imagination*', he says (*Biographia Literaria*, Chapter 13), 'I consider either as primary or secondary'. These are not value judgements—the secondary, despite the high claims made for the primary imagination, is the higher faculty:

The primary imagination I hold to be the living power and prime agent of all human perception, and as a repetition in the finite mind of the eternal act of creation in the infinite I AM.

The reason for the glowing rhetoric is that Coleridge is refuting in the most impressive terms the philosophical tradition which asserted the passivity of mind. He crystallises in this sentence his whole view of the mind's energy and shaping creativity in the act of perception. Even to perceive, is god-like.

But it is the secondary imagination which the poet employs. This faculty coexists with 'the conscious will'. It is 'identical with the primary in the *kind* of its agency' but different in degree and mode of operation.

It dissolves, diffuses, dissipates, in order to recreate; ... it struggles to idealize and unify. It is essentially vital, even as all objects (as objects) are essentially fixed and dead.

*A detailed explication of this passage is given by I. A. Richards in *The Portable Coleridge*, The Viking Press, New York, 1950; Penguin Books, Harmondsworth, 1977, pp.45–50.

If perception (primary imagination) is a *repetition* of God's creation, the secondary imagination is able to *modify* or even to *augment* that creation. It recreates Creation, re-moulding the data of perception into new forms and unities.

The term 'Imagination' becomes useful in criticism as a result of Coleridge's next sentence, which defines another poetic faculty, the 'Fancy':

> *Fancy,* on the contrary, has no other counters to play with, but fixities and definites. The Fancy is indeed no other than a mode of memory emancipated from the order of time and space; and blended with, and modified by ... choice. But equally with the ordinary memory, it must receive all its materials ready made from the law of association.

All that the Fancy does is rearrange ready-made images. This is a creative act in itself, but of lower worth. Most verse may be the product of the Fancy, but true poetry requires Imagination.

Consider this simile: 'And, like a lobster boiled, the morn / From black to red began to turn'. As Basil Willey points out,* the association between lobsters and the morning sky is vivid and amusing—but it is merely a juxtaposition of the Fancy, in which neither image is modified by the lines. True Imagination can make itself felt in the resonance of a single word. Wordsworth's favourite example was his own line: 'Over his own sweet voice the Stock-dove broods'. Here he explains why he wrote 'broods' instead of 'coos' (the usual verb for dove-sounds):

> ... by the intervention of the metaphor *broods,* the affections are called in by the imagination to assist in marking the manner in which the bird reiterates and prolongs her soft notes, as if herself delighting to listen to it, and participating of a still and quiet satisfaction, like that which may be supposed inseparable from the continuous process of incubation.

'To brood', your dictionary will tell you, means either to meditate or to sit on eggs while incubating them. Wordsworth's metaphor lets us 'see' the sounds of the dove in their rounded perfection, and visualise the warmth and softness of the bird herself, while at the same time we are aware of the whole complex image as a metaphor for the poet's meditation.

*See *Nineteenth Century Studies*, Chatto & Windus, London, 1949, p.25.

The philosophical background

Philosophical influences on Coleridge

Inescapably, what has been said about Coleridge's literary theory has involved some reference to philosophy. Since his poetry is always philosophical, it is helpful to have at least a rudimentary map of his philosophical bearings. There is not enough space in this booklet to discuss in any detail all the philosophers in whom Coleridge was interested. This section can only point out some of the major influences on his work, so that if you are interested you can follow them up by consulting full-length studies of Coleridge's thought.

Foremost of the philosophers who influenced Coleridge was *Plato*, the Greek philosopher (born 428 BC). The founder of philosophical idealism, Plato also profoundly influenced Christian thought. His philosophy is a blend of reason and mysticism. He believed that nothing in the material world is permanent, or 'real'. Knowledge, therefore, is derived not from the senses but from reason. His thought is dominated by ethical and religious considerations. At its centre is the concept of Ideas, or Forms. Behind each kind of 'appearance' in the world—a cat, a chair, a mountain—there is an Idea, eternally existent, and never wholly identical with any actually existing sample of these things. Without such an Idea, of course, conversation between human beings would be impossible—for every existing chair there would have to be a different term. We could only deal in particulars, never in general ideas. It is easy to see that this concept has a religious application. The word 'cat' refers to God's design: his cat is real, whereas those we see are imperfect materialisations of the Idea, mere appearances.

Coleridge also relied upon another of Plato's concepts, his distinction between two intellectual faculties, Reason and Understanding. The Reason is concerned with Ideas, the Understanding with perceptions. Reason is a mode of Vision (a direct seeing of things unseen), while Understanding relies upon deduction. In his famous parable of the cave Plato illustrates how, without Reason, men remain slaves of their sense perceptions. The men in his parable live in a cave, in permanent twilight. They are bound, and they sit with their backs to a fire and their faces to a wall. Seeing only shadows, they mistake them for realities: they can have no conception of the realities which cause the shadows that they see.

Like many other thinkers, Coleridge approached Plato's 'dear gorgeous nonsense', as he affectionately called it, through the Roman philosopher *Plotinus* (AD 204–70). From St Augustine (345–430)—Bishop of Hippo—onwards, Christian thought was largely built on Plotinus's representation of Plato's ideas—or Neoplatonism. Plotinus, like Plato, turned away from the shadows of our world to contemplate a word of eternal goodness and beauty. In his case, the goal was the eternal world of Ideas: to Christian theologians this other world is Heaven. The peak of Plotinus's metaphysics is a spiritual triad: the One, Spirit, and Soul. 'The One' is a term applied to what others call God—the ground of the good and the beautiful. 'Spirit' might be termed the 'intellectual' principle—either the 'Idea' of man's mind and soul at its most god-like, or that aspect of 'the One' which man may 'see' in a state of religious ecstasy. 'Soul' does not mean man's soul, but the creator of the visible world, a world which was, to Plotinus, beautiful and (as in 'The Ancient Mariner') inhabited by spirits. Plotinus also made explicit the implication in Plato's thought that the human soul is immortal, because it belongs to the eternal world of Ideas.

In England in the seventeenth and eighteenth centuries there was a native tradition of Neoplatonism, represented by such men as John Smith (1618–52) and Benjamin Whichcote (1609–88)—the 'Cambridge Platonists'—whose spiritual successor Coleridge was. But the dominant names in British philosophy are those of John Locke (1632–1704), George Berkeley (1685–1753), David Hartley (1705–57) and David Hume (1711–76)—in whom, says Coleridge, he could not find 'an abiding place for my reason' (*Biographia Literaria*, Chapter 9).

John Locke was the founder of British Empiricism, that mode of philosophy which relies upon observation and experiment rather than theory. His *Essay Concerning Human Understanding* (1690) propounds the thesis that all knowledge is derived from sense perceptions—an idea to which Coleridge became wholly opposed as it denied intuition and imagination (or Reason as Coleridge uses the word). Not only did Coleridge think Locke's reputation 'wholly unmerited'; he believed that 'any system built on the passiveness of the mind must be false as a system' (letter to Poole, 23 March 1801).

Along with Locke's 'sandy sophisms' Coleridge came to dismiss the work of David Hartley. Hartley's *Observations on Man* (1744) propounds a theory of the 'association of ideas' which, for a time, Coleridge accepted absolutely. Basically, Hartley's work is a mechanical description of the nervous system. When we perceive something, the nervous system 'vibrates': each vibration leaves a trace, a 'vibratiuncle', and the memory depends on these traces which, when reactivated, tend to reactivate each other. From associations of such sensory traces all our reasoning results. We have no will or choice in the matter of perceptions. And since our habits and values are formed by repeated pleasurable or unpleasurable stimuli, it is 'necessity'—not choice—that directs our moral and intellectual life. 'I have,' wrote Coleridge in March 1801, 'overthrown the doctrine of association as taught by Hartley, and with it all the irreligious metaphysics of modern infidels—especially the doctrine of necessity'.

David Hume carried these ideas to their logical conclusion in his *Treatise of Human Nature*, 1740. Setting out to construct a truly empirical philosophy, testing every hypothesis with scrupulous care, his work is the last word in scepticism. We can know nothing, either of the physical world or of moral values. He was both supremely logical as a thinker, and basically insincere in his philosophical position—holding, for instance, conventional moral views for which he had proved there could be no justification.

George Berkeley, whose *Principles of Human Knowledge* (1710) denied the existence of matter (and whose surname Coleridge gave to his second son) remained congenial to Coleridge long after he had rejected Locke and Hartley. Berkeley maintained that what we perceive is not 'matter' but mental qualities. Sensation cannot be the basis of mind, and to assert that it is must lead to materialism. Berkeley's denial of matter is of course a logical, not a practical step. He knew that the world existed, but for him the only guarantee of this is that God exists and that God is good (that is, he is not given to playing practical jokes on his creatures).

By and large, what passed for philosophy in the England of Locke and Hume was a compound of materialism and scepticism. Strangely, perhaps, the Utilitarian philosophers of the nineteenth century—Jeremy Bentham (1748–1832), James Mill (1773–1836) and John Stuart Mill (1806–73)—though significant in the growth of British socialism, were followers of the school of Locke. Their ignorance (except in the case of John Stuart Mill) of alternative philosophical traditions, and their contempt for Platonic philosophy and the new German Idealism, explain why Coleridge was so adamantly opposed to Reformist and Utilitarian ideas. Their Atheism, too, linked them with Locke and the philosophers of the French Revolution.

Coleridge turned to Germany to find philosophers who spoke his language. He was first attracted by the mystic Jakob Boehme (1575–1624) and the pantheist Benedict Spinoza (1632–77). Both are warmly mentioned in *Biographia Literaria*. Boehme, he said, was one of those whose writings 'contributed to keep alive the heart in the head; gave me an indistinct, yet striving and working presentiment that all the products of the mere reflective faculty partook of death'. It was the nobility and visionary quality of Boehme that appealed to him, while in Spinoza he admired these qualities allied to a deeply logical mind.

Spinoza was Coleridge's greatest temptation. His *Ethics* deals with metaphysics and psychology as well as ethics, and in all three areas is intellectually impressive. To Spinoza there is only one substance, 'God' or 'Nature'. God is infinite and includes the attributes of thought and of extension. Everything that exists is an aspect of the divine. The aim of life is an increase in consciousness of oneness with God: one must free oneself from intellectual error and selfish passions in order to obtain both wisdom and happiness. 'The mind's highest good is the knowledge of God'. The Romantic sense that all men are One Man is present in Spinoza's idea that selfish passions are divisive, while Reason is unifying. It is a large part of wisdom to see one's own misfortunes calmly and within the perspective of all humanity and all eternity, as mere details of the universal harmony. Coleridge was certainly a Spinozist at one stage, while his friend Wordsworth was arguably a Spinozist all his life: to a Romantic poet Spinozist philosophy came naturally. Yet Coleridge was a sharp enough thinker to diagnose Spinozism as Pantheism, and to reject it as incompatible with Christian belief. To the Pantheist, God is immanent in creation, and creation is deified. The Christian, however, refuses to *identify* God with Nature.

Immanuel Kant (1724–1804) was the greatest contemporary influence on Coleridge: his works, such as the *Critique of Pure Reason* (1781), 'took possession of me as with a giant's hand'. Kant's new Idealism, developed (and distorted) by Fichte and Schelling, was not identical to Coleridge's later views, but at least it appeared to refute successfully the ideas of Locke. Kant's followers, the German Romantic Idealists, were in some ways close to Berkeley. They tended to deny the objective world altogether, and rejoice in pure, liberated subjectivity: if the world was only what they imagined, so much the better. Kant's own position is more sober. Recognising the inadequacy of empiricism, he claims that the mind's knowledge of the world does not depend upon its being shaped by outer objects, but vice versa: objects conform to the structures of the mind. He asserts too (Platonically) that there are two kinds of knowledge: the partial knowledge we acquire through our experience of sense perception (Understanding); and the real knowledge of the intellect (Reason).

Another part of Kant's appeal to Coleridge was his emphasis on the moral life. Kant held that empirical reasoning does not supply moral values. The Understanding is competent to deal only with the material. In Kant, Coleridge found support for his view that if the wrong *kind* of thought is applied to morals 'the more strictly logical the reasoning is . . . the more irrational it is'. We are assured by the very structure of the mind and the conscience (not by observable phenomena) that God, free will, intuition, the conviction of immortality, are essential postulates of the moral life. Kant supplied a philosophical basis for the reassertion of the necessity of faith (belief in what cannot be proved—or disproved) to a life lived in accordance with higher Reason.

The development of Coleridge's thought

Coleridge's mind was searching and speculative, but he was concerned above all with the practical consequences, for the moral life, of his speculation. In his career he read almost everything, and at one time or another believed almost everything. We have seen how he passed through Godwinist thought, Lockean and Hartleyan philosophy, the mystics and the Neoplatonists, Unitarian and Trinitarian theology, Berkeley and Spinoza. But he was not merely an enthusiastic reader, adopting whatever views he came across in print.

The heart of his philosophical progress is the development of a model of the mind in which two separate faculties must be recognised: Reason and Understanding—the philosophical equivalent of his critical distinction between Imagination and Fancy. Indeed they are two sides of the same distinction: Wordsworth called the Imagination 'Reason in her most exalted mood'.

Reason is 'pure and impersonal', unaffected by our selfish passions or by natural or acquired habits of understanding. Coleridge describes it as the latent presence of God in us—'something in which we are, not which is in us'. It is an inward beholding of spiritual realities which we apprehend directly, just as our senses apprehend material things. It is 'the organ of the supersensuous', just as the eye is the organ of light. It sees the 'whole' rather than individual phenomena, and deals with ultimate ends. The pure sciences, mathematics, metaphysics and ethics, are the province of Reason.

Understanding is 'the science of phenomena' and gives us merely 'abstract knowledge' of things, as opposed to a substantial sense of the 'one Life' of which we are a part. The Understanding classifies, analyses, measures, and relies on our separation as subjects from the objects we observe. Its proper concerns are the physical sciences (though without Reason the scientist will be unable to direct his Understanding). When man attempts to use 'the forms and mechanisms of his mere reflective faculty' to probe into spiritual truths (the error of the Empiricist tradition) he is attempting to measure nature and divinity with inadequate tools. For if ultimate mysteries are 'cut and squared for the comprehension of the understanding' the result is 'a universe of death'. Man ends in scepticism and irreligion.

> The philosophy of mechanism ... strikes Death, and cheats itself by mistaking clear images for distinct conceptions, and idly demands conceptions where intuitions alone are possible or adequate to the majesty of the Truth.

The aim of Coleridge's philosophy (and of his unwritten great work) was to give philosophical support to the orthodox Christian conception of the Trinity of God—the Father (man's creator), the Son (man's redeemer) and the Holy Spirit (man's comforter)—and to show the necessity of this conception. If this seems unenterprising, one must remember that the whole force of the British philosophical tradition was tending toward scepticism. The most attractive counter-philosophy, in Boehme and Spinoza, was unacceptable to Coleridge because of its Pantheistic heresy—and the fashionable German thinkers, Schelling and Fichte, were under Spinoza's spell.

Coleridge aimed to present a marriage of Platonism and Christian thought, and to show that Christianity was not merely desirable but philosophically *true*. In this apparently conservative position, there is a forward-looking element. Coleridge's religion was not merely one of the head, though it did have to satisfy his very keen intellect. When he defends the idea of the Trinity he does so because a *personal* God is necessary to him—a God, that is, whom one can address as 'Thou'. A number of modern theologians (most notably the Jewish philosopher Martin Buber) assume that one of the fundamentals of human life is the possibility of an 'I-Thou' relationship between man and man, man and God, man and nature. Coleridge is one of the originators of this idea, though in his case the concept is related to his belief in the Trinity. To Coleridge, the Trinity of God is essential because God, in order to be a *personal* God, must be able to say 'Thou'—or he would not be an 'I'. 'There can be no I [logically speaking] without a Thou', he wrote. Since this is a philosophical idea, it is as true of God as it is of man.

Coleridge's religion, then, is not abstract. It arises from a deep human need—a conviction that without God he is nothing. Either he is upheld by God, or there is only nothingness.

The impact of Coleridge on Victorian thought was immense. In so far as Christianity was able to fight a rearguard action, and even to recover ground after the onslaught of atheism, Coleridge is one of the thinkers who inspired that resistance. His work was out of step with the main figures in formal British philosophy, yet later in the nineteenth century John Stuart Mill had to recognise that his was one of the seminal minds of the age. The language of religious, ethical and social thought—as well as that of criticism—is still responding to Coleridge's influence.

Early nature poetry

In 'Sonnet: to the River Otter', 'The Eolian Harp' and 'Reflections on Having left a Place of Retirement' we are now in a position to observe how Coleridge is developing his own poetic voice under the influence of such poets as Bowles and Akenside, and how these poems reflect such philosophical influences as Associationism, Neoplatonism, Platonism and the Spinozistic 'one Life'.

The subject of 'To the River Otter' is the association of ideas. The mode of writing is based upon Bowles's sonnet 'To the River Itchin'. Bowles, in his sonnet, briefly describes the river and then asks why he feels pain whenever he revisits it. He suggests three reasons—the passage of time, the end of youth, and the loss of friends. His poem concludes by referring to the solace he obtains from the river, which is itself a long-lost friend. Coleridge's poem is more lively than this. His evocation of the river scene is more vivid in colour and sharper in detail. His emotional state is more complex. Coleridge is not simply attaching his reflections to a scene; he is clearly *experiencing* mingled nostalgia and delight. The solace of the river is demonstrated by the way its waters 'rise' in memory, and the clarity of memory is ingeniously suggested by the clarity of the brook itself as Coleridge remembers it. The pictorial sharpness also persuades us of the depth of the original impression, and if the memory were not 'deep' (line 5) it could not 'rise' (line 8). Finally the desire to be 'a careless child' is made more convincing by the depicting of such a child in line 4. The mental traffic is two-way: consolation is brought from the past, yet turns into nostalgia for that past. This double mode of melancholy is redeemed by the poem's sense of movement, colour, and mental energy.

Mingled in the texture of 'The Eolian Harp' are ideas which suggest Plotinus (with his world-soul and musical harmony), Berkeley's way of seeing phenomena as mental qualities, and even Spinoza's belief in the one substance of nature and divinity. However dubious Coleridge may have been about the content of lines 44–8, he constantly quoted them with delight, and in a sense reinforced them by the late addition of lines 26–33. Certainly the lines powerfully suggest man's unity with the rest of the created world—a unity which can be grasped only by Reason and Imagination, not by the reflective Understanding. The 'whole man' participates; his Understanding merely reflects. Perhaps the disunity of the poem illustrates the division between head and heart, for at this stage Coleridge's religious thought is in conflict with his deeper intuitions, and it is on a note of orthodox reflection that the poem ends.

'Reflections' also exhibits an inner conflict. But here the conflict is between the attractions of meditation (still, in lines 38–40, dangerously Spinozist) and the 'categorical imperative' (to use Kant's term) of engagement in human affairs. Even the phrase in line 60—'I therefore go and *join head, heart, and hand* ... to fight the bloodless fight'—is intended philosophically. To Coleridge, philosophy was not worthy of the name if it did not combine reflection, feeling and will, to issue in action. Coleridge is here making an existential choice and commitment.

Of these three poems the most perfect is clearly the sonnet. The other, more conversational poems, do not yet have sufficient consistency of style or structure. Yet if they are compared with minor poetry of the period, or with Coleridge's more conventional work at that time (such as 'The Faded Flower' or 'Addressed to a Young Man of Fortune' they stand out as experiments in expressing a new kind of awareness of man's interrelation with nature.

The conversation poems

Form

'This Lime-tree Bower', 'Frost at Midnight' and 'The Nightingale' are the finest examples of a form Coleridge invented: the 'conversation poem', or 'poems of friendship'. 'The Eolian Harp' also belongs to this group, and 'Reflections', 'To William Wordsworth', 'Fears in Solitude', the verse 'Letter to Sara Hutchinson' and even 'The Pains of Sleep' share some of the characteristics of the form. The critic G. M. Harper was the first to apply the term 'conversation poem', which Coleridge uses only in 'The Nightingale', in this wider sense. Other critics prefer to include these poems in a broader group which M. H. Abrams calls 'the greater Romantic lyric'.*

The conversation poem is a development of lyric poetry, which term we must define. Originally a lyric poem was intended to be sung, and was usually written in stanzas (groups of lines with a fixed pattern of rhyme and metre). Formally it may resemble ballad poetry, except that ballads tend to be longer. Moreover, the ballad is essentially a narrative poem—telling a story, usually objectively and in the third person—whereas the lyric is a personal utterance, expressing mood, feeling or reflection.

The Romantic poets wrote formal lyric poems (many of their sonnets, ballads and songs are lyrical) but they favoured a hybrid form in which lyrical mood and subject are combined with blank verse. Blank verse may be defined as unrhymed iambic pentameter: that is, a sequence of lines of ten syllables each, in which the basic metre is iambic—alternating unstressed syllables with stressed:

To sit | beside | our Cot, | our Cot, | o'ergrown

Of course, no one reads an iambic lines as regularly as that, and it is unusual, especially in Romantic lyric poetry, to find many lines which are exactly iambic, even in theory. The first line of 'This Lime-tree Bower' is not scanned as

Well they are gone and here must I remain

but as

Well, they are gone, and here must I remain.

In fact, in the natural cadence of the line, one does not hear 'well' and 'gone' as identical: 'well' is a rising tone, while 'gone' is falling. The 'I' is less prominent than 'here' and 'remain'. Also, a meaningful pause in a line

---

*G. M. Harper's essay 'Coleridge's Conversation Poems' appears in *English Romantic Poets*, edited by M. H. Abrams, 2nd edition, Oxford University Press, Oxford, 1975.

may replace one of the expected stresses. So we could read the line as follows (′ = primary stress; ` = secondary stress; ∧ = pause):

Well, they are gone ∧ and here must I remain.

The placing of that pause, however, is a free choice in this line (it could come after 'well'). In general you will find five stresses to a line, but one or more of these may be silent, and may occur between the lines. Counting stresses rather than syllables our first example becomes:

To sit beside our Cot ∧ our Cot o'ergrown.

There are no mechanical rules for reading English blank verse. 'This Lime-tree Bower' can be said to include lines as various as this:

Well ∧ they are gone, and here must I remain,

This lime-tree bower my prison! ∧ I have lost

Beauty and feelings ∧ such as would have been

Most sweet to my remembrance ∧ even when age

Had dimmed mine eyes to blindness! ∧ They, meanwhile,

Friends ∧ whom I never more may meet again,

∧On springy heath, along the hill-top edge

Wander in gladness ∧ and wind down perchance

To that still roaring dell of which I told;

∧The roaring dell, o'erwooded, narrow, deep

∧And only speckled by the mid-day sun.

But the conversation poems are not always written in such relaxed cadence. In the early poems—'The Eolian Harp', for instance—one sees interference from earlier verse styles. Lyrical blank verse is best when the units of sense do not coincide with the line endings; when, that is, the lines are 'run-on', as they are in the first lines of 'Reflections' (line 7 is the only 'end-stopped' line in the first paragraph of that poem).

In lines 26–33 of 'The Eolian Harp', the verse (though fine and memorable) is formal in an eighteenth-century manner. The favourite verse for philosophical poetry in the eighteenth century was the rhymed 'heroic couplet'. You will see that Coleridge has really written four unrhymed couplets (eight lines) in which the division of sense is made even more rhetorical by the use of elegant parallelism within and between the lines (this pattern is strongly felt in lines 34–43 and 54–7):

O! the one Life *within* us and *abroad* [antithesis]

Which *meets* all *motion* and *becomes* its *soul* [nouns and verbs parallel]

A *light*[1] in *sound*[2] a *sound*[2]-like power in *light*[1] [two reversed terms]

Rhythm[1] in *all*[2] thought and *joyance*[1] *everywhere*[2] [parallelism with semantic echoes]

Lines 5 and 6 of the same poem illustrate another legacy of earlier verse, the habit of using images as emblems of abstract qualities:

> With white flower'd Jasmin, and the broad-leav'd Myrtle
> (Meet emblems they of Innocence and Love!).

In many of his lesser poems, early and late, Coleridge relapses into this style, with its thundering capitalised terms:

> Whilst pale Anxiety, corrosive Care,
> Tear of Woe, the gloom of sad Despair
> And deepen'd Anguish generous bosoms rend. . . .

Coleridge's best poetry is almost wholly free of this habit, though he never really shared his friend Wordsworth's distaste for 'poetic diction' (he thought 'Religious Musings' was one of his best poems).

Other characteristics

The development of a freer conversational cadence is not the only characteristic of the conversation poems. They are written in the style of intimate talk to an understanding auditor, and in most cases we know who the imagined addressee is. The poems are addressed to his wife (early in their marriage), to William and Dorothy Wordsworth, to Charles Lamb, to his son Hartley, and to Sara Hutchinson. This is far from being a formal gesture. Coleridge had a great gift for friendship, and a great need for it. He wrote in a letter: 'Man is truly altered by the coexistence of other men; his faculties cannot be developed in himself alone, and only by himself'. His friends inspired powerful emotions in him, and grateful meditation on such emotions is part of his strategy for deepening his own self-awareness. That is not to say that the poems are self-centred, for one of their most striking characteristics is the generous, loving spirit we feel in them all.

In discussing lyric poetry we sometimes speak of a 'lyric persona', when it seems improper to identify the speaker with the poet. In these poems, however, the speaker is undoubtedly Coleridge himself: this unambivalent identity is one of the distinguishing features of the conversation poems. Furthermore, we know the precise biographical context of the poems, sometimes because we are explicitly told what the context is, and sometimes because it is easily inferred. The poems are usually about Coleridge in a particular state of mind, at a particular time. So speaker, auditor, and biographical context are made unusually explicit.

Further, we have in each poem a precise specification of space and time. Sometimes the place and date of composition are stated: this habit was shared by all the Romantic poets, as in Shelley's 'Stanzas written in Dejection, near Naples', or Wordsworth's 'Lines written a few miles above Tintern Abbey on revisiting the banks of the Wye during a tour, July 13, 1798'. More characteristic of Coleridge is the care with which he specifies the time of day, the atmosphere, his exact surroundings, so that each poem has an easily visualised setting. It is not that he wants a picturesque frame for his meditation. Rather, the peculiar quality of these poems is that the landscape, or fireside, or nocturnal sounds, or garden sights, stimulate the meditation that takes place and help to influence the direction his thoughts take. When a dramatic change occurs in the course of the poem it may be caused by some train of association in the poet's mind, or by a freak of memory, or by something outside him altogether: inner and outer are partners in the process. Remember that Coleridge thought of art as 'the reconciler of nature and man'. In these poems he comes closest to fulfilling his poetic aim of 'infusing the thoughts and passions of man into everything which is the object of his contemplation' and reconciling 'what is nature with that which is exlusively human'.

This naturalness does not make the poems random or artless. Usually they have a satisfying shape—in the sense that the movement of thought circles or spirals around a given theme or image, while recording some kind of progress, either in insight or in the release of emotional pressure. Coleridge thought that the art of narrative was to reconcile the linear flow of experience with the satisfactions of form. Usually in the conversation poems his solution is to come full circle at the end, recycling the opening imagery with added significance or subtle variation.

Before you read on, take time to read through the conversation poems and consider to what extent they each possess the above characteristics.

'Reflections' and 'Frost at Midnight' compared

When we move from 'The Eolian Harp' to 'This Lime-tree Bower', or from 'Reflections on Having Left a Place of Retirement' to 'Frost at Midnight', we are likely to feel that the poetry is of a higher order. All are good poems, but those which were written later are masterpieces, while the poems of 1795 are, by comparison, rough prototypes, What can we observe in detail to substantiate this judgement?

In 'Reflections' Coleridge is reflecting on the scene he presents, summarising his experience in somewhat general terms. The presence of Sara is stated in the presentation of the past, but is not active in the poem. The detail of the cottage is not particularly sharp, and the setting is rather abstractly presented as 'the Valley of Seclusion'. Bristol is poetically called 'Bristowa'; the merchant is 'a son of commerce', an allegorical figure whose 'thirst for gold' (which may be a totally unfair judgement on the stranger) needs to be calmed by nature. The skylark is made the subject of a formal, moralising simile (19–26). The mount is also allegorically used, and unrealistically described. Remnants of poetic cliché and rhetoric appear in the third paragraph: 'on rose-leaf beds, pampering the coward heart', 'the sluggard Pity's vision-weaving tribe', 'the bloodless fight/ Of Science, Freedom and the Truth in Christ'.

There is at the end of the poem the 'return' to the opening subject, which is common to the structure of all the conversation poems. But the reiteration of five words from the opening lines (Cot, Jasmin, Rose, Myrtle and sea) is purely formal. Only the sea has figured at all in the meditation. We are unlikely to feel that the repetition expresses more than nostalgia.

'Frost at Midnight' begins with an image of present activity and proceeds to specify very precisely the atmosphere in which the meditation is taking place, and by which it is heightened. The co-presence of the sleeping baby and the 'ministry' of the frost is felt throughout the poem. The thoughts in the poem—whether about frost, or the moon, or the sooty film—are not ready-made and merely 'hung' on the peg of an appropriate image. The frosty calm is vexing the poet's meditation. The sooty film mirrors the poet's unquiet soul, and provides a direction for his thoughts. Paragraph two is caused by the imagery of paragraph one. The 'eternal language, which thy God/ Utters' (60–1) has already been demonstrated by such communicative images. Finally, when we return to the 'secret ministry' of frost at the end of the poem, not only does Coleridge intensify the effect by the uniquely beautiful personification, but the meaning of 'ministry' has been deepened by the meditation of lines 44–64 stressing nature's moulding of the spirit. There is, too, a change of image, from the coals of the dying fire, which lead the poet's thoughts inwards, to the radiance of the moon—the timeless element in that night landscape.

The poem is marked by its subtlety in following the course of the poet's thought, which is at once intimate and yet concerned with vastnesses of time and space—past, present and future; earth and heaven. From the soot on the grate to the quiet moon, we are kept conscious of the moulding, shaping elements of nature and their 'sympathies' with each other and with man. The images are invested with clarity and separateness, but they are also unified in a felt harmony.

Political poems

As a public poet Coleridge remained more conventional in his style. We tend to value the last of his political poems, 'Fears in Solitude' (April 1798), the most highly because it has much of the flexibility of the conversation poems. It shares their specific location, their sense of attachment to a particular place and the people in it. The mode of the poem is confessional rather than rhetorical: the poem reflects Coleridge's own troubled state of mind as he vacillates between radicalism and patriotism, trying to reconcile these conflicting elements.

How successful this approach is may be tested most easily by comparing 'Fears in Solitude' with two earlier effusions, 'Religious Musings' (1794) and 'The Destiny of Nations' (1796). 'Religious Musings' is an impersonal interpretation of the events of the age (in particular the French Revolution) in the light of Christian scripture, mingled with some explicitly Hartleyan and Berkeleyan philosophy. The basic theme is the popular conviction of the time that the French Revolution heralded the Millennium: the amazing political events in France convinced many people that the Apocalypse, as foretold in the book of Revelation (the last book of the Bible), was at hand. Only the most dedicated literary scholars find this poem at all readable, yet buried in it (awaiting the more 'appropriate form' of the conversation poems) are a number of lines with which you should be familiar. Lines 45–51, 114–22, 135–40 and 414–19 are among Coleridge's most explicit verse statements on the nature of God and the destiny of the soul. Viewed as Christian doctrine they are very radical, a blend of Boehme, Berkeley and Spinoza, rather than of orthodox Church dogma.

Similarly, lines 13–35 of 'The Destiny of Nations' are a good summary of Coleridge's Christian Platonism. In the later part of the poem, the 'machinery' (the poem is a vision manipulated by tutelary spirits) and some of the descriptions, especially in lines 363–70 and 470–4, suggest the kind of poetry Coleridge would write in 'The Ancient Mariner'. But 'The Destiny of Nations' is not, as a whole, a poem that many people can read with pleasure.

Coleridge's political output includes two odes: 'Ode to the Departing Year' (1796) and 'France: an Ode' (1798). The earlier poem is full of bombastic rhetoric and stanzas which Coleridge has to explain in the 'argument'. The later ode, though formal, has the substantial merit of concerning itself not with grand visionary statements but with Coleridge's own feelings upon the occasion.

It is ironical that of the three effusions and two odes mentioned here— all dealing with the revolutionary situation in France—the most convincing and the most radical as poems are those of 1798, the poems in which he expresses his recantation of revolutionary views.

Coleridge and the *Lyrical Ballads*

In Chapter 14 of *Biographia Literaria* Coleridge recalls how the *Lyrical Ballads* project was conceived:

The thought suggested itself (to which of us I do not recollect) that a series of poems might be composed of two sorts. In the one, the incidents and agents were to be, in part at least, supernatural; and the excellence aimed at was to consist in the interesting of the affections by the dramatic truth of such emotions as would naturally accompany such situations, supposing them real. And real in this sense they have been to every human being who, from whatever source of delusion, has at any time believed himself under supernatural agency. For the second class, subjects were to be chosen from ordinary life....

In this idea originated the plan of the *Lyrical Ballads*; in which it was agreed that my endeavours should be directed to persons and characters supernatural, or at least romantic; yet so as to transfer from our inward nature a human interest and a semblance of truth sufficient to procure for these shadows of imagination that willing suspension of disbelief for the moment, which constitutes poetic faith. Mr Wordsworth, on the other hand, was to propose to himself as his object to give the charm of novelty to things of every day, and to excite a feeling analogous to the supernatural by awakening the mind's attention from the lethargy of custom and directing it to the loveliness and the wonders of the world before us; an inexhaustible treasure, but for which, in consequence of the film of familiarity and selfish solicitude, we have eyes yet see not, ears that hear not, and hearts that neither feel nor understand.

With this view I wrote the 'Ancient Mariner', and was preparing, among other poems, the 'Dark Ladie', and the 'Christabel', in which I should have more nearly realized my ideal than I had done in my first attempt.

This is an admirable statement of the division of labour between the two poets, in theory at least. What Coleridge says about his own and Wordsworth's modes of poetry is very exact—and his comments on Wordsworth apply also to his own conversation poems. Oddly, of the five poems which Coleridge contributed to *Lyrical Ballads*, only one, 'The Ancient Mariner', was a ballad, and it is really this poem which his words here describe. His other contributions were 'The Nightingale', 'Love', and the two extracts from his play *Osorio*—'The Foster-Mother's Tale' and 'The Dungeon'.

The surprising thing about *Lyrical Ballads* is that the project ever got off the ground. Wordsworth's appreciation of 'The Ancient Mariner' was muted. Coleridge disapproved of many of Wordsworth's poems, including a number of the most famous. Although the Preface to the second edition of *Lyrical Ballads*, one of the major critical documents in English literature, was written by Wordsworth at Coleridge's request, he found a good deal in it to disagree with. As he wrote to Southey in 1802 'I rather suspect that ... there is a radical difference in our theoretical opinions respecting Poetry'. In *Biographia Literaria* he devoted two chapters to criticising Wordsworth's theory that poetry should be written in 'a selection of the real language of men' and his practice of writing poems about 'low and rustic life'. Wordsworth's aim was to write poems which would dramatise the experience of ordinary people, and to do so, as far as possible, in language suited to the people in the poems. Coleridge's view of poetry was both more ideal and more traditional: 'I adopt with full faith the principle of Aristotle that poetry as poetry is essentially ideal, that it avoids and excludes all accident ... and that the persons of poetry must be clothed ... with the common attributes of the class'. Wordsworth's willingness to deal directly with the unpleasant and the naturally abnormal—with swollen ankles and mental defectiveness for example—was not to Coleridge's taste at all. When Coleridge published a ballad poem called 'The Three Graves' (partly Wordsworth's conception) he prefaced it with an apology for its language, explaining that he does not regard it as a poem:

> The language was intended to be dramatic; that is, suited to the narrator; and the metre corresponds to the homeliness of the diction. It is presented therefore as the fragment, not of a Poem, but of a common Ballad-tale. Whether this is sufficient to justify the adoption of such a style, in any metrical composition not professedly ludicrous, the Author is himself in some doubt. At all events, it is not presented as poetry, and it is in no way connected with the Author's judgement concerning poetic diction.

In his other ballads, from the first version of 'The Ancient Mariner' to 'Alice du Clos' (1828), Coleridge's preference was for imitating the metre and diction of older ballads and placing them in the realm of Romance or the supernatural. His aim is 'to elevate the imagination and set the affections in right tune by the beauty of the inanimate impregnated as with a living soul by the presence of life' (letter to his brother, April 1798).

Coleridge's 'divine comedy'

This term, used by the critic G. Wilson Knight to describe 'The Ancient Mariner', 'Christabel', and 'Kubla Khan',* suggests that these three poems correspond to the *Purgatorio, Inferno,* and *Paradiso* in the Italian

*In *The Starlit Dome*, Methuen, London, 1941, p.83.

poet Dante's *Divina Commedia*. Whether 'Christabel' would have amounted to a full portrait of Hell is hard to tell, but 'The Ancient Mariner' is certainly purgatorial, and 'Kubla Khan' intertwines a number of visions of Paradise.

The three poems are also unified by their dream-like quality. They are all instances of the most imaginative kind of poetry, concerning nightmarish or visionary experience, or both. They all have, also, a close relation to the imagery of Coleridge's own dreams, and each poem touches upon aspects of Coleridge's conception of the poet. The tale of 'The Ancient Mariner' has been seen as an allegory of the poet's curse, in that the poet, too, surrenders domestic tranquillity in order to undergo strange visions, whose content it is his fate to preach. In 'Christabel' those visions are of peculiar horror; in 'Kubla Khan' they suggest the blessedness of the poet's role. Bard Bracy, the Mariner, and the prophet-figure in 'Kubla Khan' are all projections of Coleridge himself—the dreamer of these dreams and visions.

'The Ancient Mariner'

The verse form of 'The Ancient Mariner' is a subtle modification of traditional ballad-metre—a modification which Coleridge found in the ballad 'Sir Cauline' in Percy's *Reliques of Ancient English Poetry*. The norm is a four-line stanza, with alternating eight- and six-syllable iambic lines, full rhyme in the second and fourth lines and partial rhyme in the first and third. But stanzas of five and six lines appear, and one stanza has nine lines. These appear at moments of particular tension, or when the pressure of the narrative delays the close of the stanza. Nor is the number of syllables constant. Even the first stanza has irregularities in the second and third lines, though the second stanza is regular. As in the conversation poems, it is the stresses, not the syllables, that count. To the eye, the third line of the poem has two extra syllables, but they do not upset the four-stress pattern of the line:

By thy long grey beard and glittering eye.

There are places in the poem where, in one's reading, it seems right to replace one of the stresses by a pause, but in general the hypnotic quality of this metre is best realised by keeping to the regular alternation of three and four stresses to each line:

Water, water, every where
Nor any drop to drink

If the substantive words in each line are stressed, the stanzas will usually fall easily into a 4–3–4–3 pattern:

A speck, a mist, a shape, I wist!
And still it neared and neared:
As if it dodged a water-sprite,
It plunged and tacked and veered.

Part of the flavour of this ballad comes from Coleridge's use of occasional archaic terms, such as 'eftsoons', 'swound', 'weal', or outmoded pieties as in 'Heaven's Mother send us grace'. These add a sense of historical authenticity, although the language of the poem as a whole does not accurately reflect any actual period. Originally the poem was fuller of such archaisms to the point of quaintness. In revision, Coleridge first removed them all, and then reinstated just enough of them to differentiate his language from everyday usage.

He also introduced, in a late revision, the device of marginal glosses, which contribute to the effect of the poem and help to emphasise that it belongs to an unusual dimension of experience—one that has to be interpreted to us. In a poem in which the metre tends to hurry us along, and the plot is eventful and gripping, the scenes exotic and compelling, we may tend to read it unreflectingly. The glosses call our attention to matters of particular significance. At the beginning they simply summarise events; only the last gloss in Part 1 expresses a judgement. Some of the glosses—for instance those at lines 120, 131 and 393—help to clarify the text. But their main use is to interpret the narrative from a more meditative point of view than that of the Mariner. For instance, the phrase 'a dear ransom' (line 160) adds an emotive gloss to the Mariner's matter-of-fact narration at this point. The longer gloss at 263–6 intensifies the Mariner's experience by importing Coleridge's own response to the beauty of the night sky, and his own sense of being excluded from its joyful harmony. Often these glosses rephrase the experience of the poem in such a way as to express Coleridge's own insights and values more directly—though in a style which is as formal, and fictional, as the poem itself.

The enduring appeal of the poem lies in its vividness of presentation of a strange world, sometimes hauntingly beautiful, sometimes terrifying, just beyond the threshold of our own. It is not just the presence of spirits and seraphs that makes the poem magical, but the endless strokes of genius in describing actual sights of the world of common experience with imaginative intensity—

As idle as a painted ship
Upon a painted ocean ...

The water, like a witch's oils,
Burnt green, and blue and white ...

The steersman's face by his lamp gleamed white;
From the sails the dew did drip. . . .

Not only is this a world of clear, simple images in primary colours; the emotions and situations are primary too. The sense of adventure at the start, the vacillations of the crew, the fear and the yearning, the blessedness of sleep, the joy of homecoming, the momentary impulses, the desire to be understood, all these are human universals. The Mariner himself is not gifted with special wisdom, but he lives his experience intensely. His similes ('like the whizz of my cross-bow'), his direct emotional responses ('the many men so beautiful, and they all dead did lie'), his capacity for experience and his sense of the importance of that experience, whether ordinary or extraordinary, all make him the ideal narrator—the ideal bearer of a message to the Wedding-Guest from beyond the threshold on which they stand.

The poem begins with a particularly dramatic form of a characteristic Romantic moment: a confrontation in which the abnormal intrudes violently into social normality. The man who is chosen to hear the Mariner's tale is a guest at a wedding—a sacrament in which two people are united. The story he is to hear concerns the Mariner's deeper experience of the meaning of unity and love.

The world described by the Mariner is at first an ordinary one, but the terms of the description are not those of scientific observation: the universe is explicitly alive, the sun's movements, for instance, appear to be volitional. The Albatross is both natural and symbolical. In any case the symbolism is not literary, but is based on sailors' traditional belief. The Mariner's act at the end of Part 1 is a terrible violation of that belief, as well as a breach of trust. He breaks the law of love, and the killing of the Albatross may be compared to the killing of Christ (the bird is thought of by the sailors as a Christian soul, but Coleridge himself also used the 'wings of love' as a figure for God), or other literary instances of crimes against hospitality. In English literature the crime recalls the murder of Duncan by his hosts in Shakespeare's *Macbeth*: all literatures have analogous scenes.

The Mariner's act creates a world of death. Even the sun comes up upon the other side—a natural event, but the narrative makes it sound sinister. The living sea is now experienced as a desert. Water, the symbol of grace, is denied the mariners. Part 3 concerns the Mariner's increasing consciousness of guilt and isolation, followed by his selection—by the spirits—for special penance. Part 4 describes the cosmic isolation of the guilty soul, cut off by sin from the universal harmony: the moon and the stars are at home, but the Mariner's fate is to be 'Alone, alone, all all alone,/Alone on a wide wide sea'. Mysteriously, the Mariner's release is achieved by an act as involuntary as his crime; but his salvation is brought about by an act of feeling, whereas his crime was one of non-feeling. He is rewarded by the emblems of grace—water and sleep.

His return to the common world is marked by a more violent transition than his departure from it: the ship, having been manned by spirits, and having been the vehicle of unearthly experience, has no place in the world of men, and it sinks. And although the Mariner himself returns to land, he is marked by a special fatality. Like other wanderers in literature and myth—like the Flying Dutchman, or the Wandering Jew, or Cain (Coleridge was thinking at one time of writing about the travels of Cain, the first murderer), the Mariner appears to become a timeless, ghostly figure:

> I pass, like night, from land to land;
> I have strange power of speech ...

It is clear that in this poem the Mariner is exposed to 'agents ... in part at least, supernatural'. When we consider the events in the poem, and the strange timelessness of the Mariner, it is possible to wonder whether he too is not, in part at least, supernatural. At the beginning, he seems ordinary enough. But his distinguishing act—a crime against the 'one Life'—has exposed him to experience of a world beyond the ordinary. What he learns there, and is destined to preach, is the meaning and the value of what should be the ordinary sanctities of life. Would a person with such knowledge be merely unusual, or would he be positively supernatural? You might like to consider that question—though the answer probably has something to do with Coleridge's interest in the relation between our world of shadows and the bright world of eternal Ideas.

Why does the Mariner choose the Wedding-Guest to hear his tale? To this question an answer will be suggested in Part 4. Meanwhile it will be a valuable exercise for you to consider what your own answer would be.

Finally, here are four ways in which various readers see the essential meaning of 'The Ancient Mariner'. Your own interpretation may not be identical with any of these, or it may combine elements of them all. The poem has been seen as:

(a) an allegory of the fall, purgation and salvation, of the individual or of the race;

(b) a dramatisation of how imaginative vision reveals spiritual realities which cannot be grasped by understanding alone;

(c) a nightmare voyage into the irrational, akin to a nightmare of inexplicable and inescapable guilt and suffering;

(d) an existential parable, in which one man's exceptional crime and exceptional experience are rewarded by greater consciousness and vision into the meaning of existence.

'Christabel'

'Christabel', though intended for the second edition of *Lyrical Ballads*, was excluded for three reasons. Not only was it unfinished, and already promising to be too long, but, according to Coleridge, 'it was in direct opposition to the very purpose for which the lyrical ballads were published'—that is, to demonstrate that incidents of common life could provide the deepest literary interest. Yet his remark in *Biographia Literaria*, on 'The Ancient Mariner', seems equally applicable to 'Christabel', which surely does transfer 'from our inward nature a human interest and a semblance of truth sufficient to procure for the shadows of imagination that willing suspension of disbelief for the moment which constitutes poetic faith'.

Quite literally, Coleridge transfers to this poem much of his own domestic experience: the relationship between Sir Leonine and Christabel partly reflects his own relationship with his children at this time. Like Hartley, Christabel is a child of nature, and like Coleridge's children she experiences partial rejection in consequence of her father's state of mind. Presumably the complete poem would have been largely about the trial of innocence by unsuspected evil, and possibly about the redemption of evil by innocence. As it stands, the fragment shows the innocent Christabel caught between Geraldine's veiled wickedness and Sir Leonine's lack of insight. The child's only ally in the fragment is the poet, whose dream has the ring of truth. We do not know to what extent love, in the person of Christabel's betrothed knight, would have proved triumphant in the completed poem.

Beneath the fantastic surface, then, the poem deals with human universals. On the surface, too, Coleridge displays a skilful blend of symbolism and psychology. The veiled moon of line 19 looks 'both small and dull'—an indication of troubled and obscured vision which is taken up later in the poem when Christabel's eyes ('so innocent and blue') imitate Geraldine's serpent-like glance ('a snake's small eye blinks dull and shy'). In her enchantment Christabel becomes what she fears—her 'hiss' of indrawn breath, also, is both naturalistic and symbolic of the spell she is under.

The poem exhibits a conflict between some kind of embodied evil, and the girl's natural and religious grace. Geraldine is perhaps possessed by evil, rather than evil in herself. The portrait is ambiguous. We do not know whether she is to be pitied or feared, whether she will be redeemed or defeated by the forces of good. All that we have is a fascinating depiction of evil, mysterious and erotic, insinuating itself beneath Christabel's spiritual guard.

Coleridge had a technical reason for publishing the poem as a fragment in 1816. Many knew of its existence in manuscript, and two poets—Sir Walter Scott (1771–1832) and Lord Byron—had published poems influenced by the remarkable tone and metre of Coleridge's poem. He wished to place his distinctive verse before the public, and did so with a preface explaining the metrical principle; 'that of counting in each line the accents, not the syllables. Though the latter may vary from seven to twelve, yet in each line the accents will be found to be only four'. In fact there are many lines with fewer than seven syllables, and with only two or three stresses. The variation in line length gives him a more flexible medium for changes of tone and emotional quality, and the variations correspond 'with some transition in the nature of the imagery or passion'.

'Kubla Khan'

Form: A number of readers doubt whether Coleridge's most famous 'fragment' is really a fragment at all. There may have been 'a person on business from Porlock' who interrupted the composition, and the work may have been begun in an opium-induced reverie. But the poem was considerably revised in manuscript, and its artistry reflects a high degree of intellectual and poetic labour: many have had opium dreams, but there is only one 'Kubla Khan'. Unfinished it may be, but the style of this poem is not that of a long poem—an epic, a ballad, a blank verse effusion. Its form is closest to that of 'Dejection: an Ode', and it has, with visionary variations, exactly those qualities which Coleridge liked in the ode form: 'Impetuosity of Transition' and 'Precipitation of Fancy and Feeling'. Had Coleridge genuinely felt that it was incomplete, there can be little doubt that his 'recollection of the general purport of the vision ... and eight or ten scattered lines and images' would have enabled him to compose the remainder. Coleridge probably left it as it is because for 'A Vision in a Dream' this 'fragment' is the appropriate form. The gentry of Coleridge's day were given to building ruins in their parks and gardens, deliberately unfinished, open structures (open both to the elements and to imaginative interpretation), suggestive of what cannot easily be realised in a completed building—mystery and the sublime.

It may seem crude to call attention to the formal qualities of so magical a poem. But Coleridge's account of its composition tempts one to look closely at its texture: what kind of poetry is it that he composed 'in a profound sleep' and wrote down 'instantly and eagerly' on waking? It is patterned to an exquisite degree:

In Xanadu did Kubla Khan
A stately pleasure-dome decree;
Where Alph, the sacred river, ran
Through caverns measureless to man
    Down to a sunless sea.

There is alliteration of 'n', 'd' and 'k' in line one. The 'd' alliteration recurs in the second line, followed by another 'k'-sound in 'decree'. Final alliteration is common to each of the first five lines (k, d, r, m, s). Pleasure and measure, lines two and four, make an additional rhyme: they recur, incidentally, in lines 27, 31, 33 and 36 of the poem, bringing out the pleasurable association of a musical measure (tune) with measureless-ness (infinity). The single word *'measureless'*, line 4, is phonetically linked to *'man'*, *'pleasure'*, *'river'* and *'sunless sea'*. There are curiously patterned vowels: those of line 1 are i-a-a-u and i-u-a-a, while short and long vowels are related in line 2, and in line 4 each of the vowels occurs twice (the first four vowels recur in random order). The subsequent lines of the poem do not maintain this density of patterning, but if you observe such sequences as *'ground . . . girdled round'*, along with simpler alliteration and internal rhyme you will find that the verse is unusually rich throughout. In itself this does not prove conscious artistry (we alliterate as babies, and in our sleep), but the coexistence of such patterning with symbolic resonance and plain sense does not come about by accident.

Theme: There can be no single 'correct' reading of any interesting poem: 'Kubla Khan', more replete with pure symbols than most poetry, is open to a variety of interpretations. To some readers, poetry of such passionate music needs no intellectual interpretation: it satisfies simply as a hauntingly beautiful expression of the poet's longing for some ultimate beauty, combining the works of man with those of nature and those of pure imagination.

To other readers, however, such lines as

The shadow of the dome of pleasure
Floated mid-way on the waves

must, in a poem by Coleridge, embody the Platonic conception of shadows cast upon the sea of material existence by light from the world of Ideas: the whole poem, indeed, should be read as a revelation of the 'real' through symbols of the 'apparent'.

In another interpretation, the river is seen as the central symbol. It flows from a mysterious source (birth, or generation) through a 'mazy' course (the complexities of life) to sink tumultuously into 'a lifeless ocean' (the sea of death). The intensely sexual imagery of lines 16–19 support this view—the earth is procreative. Between birth and death man is overshadowed by a dream of permanence—the shadows cast by the dome of pleasure. The dome, with its 'sun' and 'ice', represents a reconciliation of opposites which is impossible to human life as it passes from fountains to a sunless sea. The reader may see Kubla as God, or god-like, in this interpretation. His creation, the dome, is an emblem of God's creation in which all that seems transient and tumultuous, to the eye of a traveller on the stream of life, is to a timeless Intelligence part of an ultimate harmony.

But is the dome to be identified with Coleridge's ideal? Other readers see Kubla as a figure of power, attempting to create something beautiful and permanent, but doomed to perish. The poet's 'But', in line 12, contrasts the planned classical artefact of Kubla with the romantic chasm, birthplace of poetic genius and true creativity. The natural scene is a more perfect symbol of the eternal because it is organic. Turmoil and flux are eternal in a way the material dome cannot be.

There are in any case two men in the poem, the other being the poet. Are there also two domes, Kubla's architectural creation and the poet's musical one? The Mount Abora of which the maiden sings is part of the landscape of Milton's paradise, and the ideal poet—we are told in the closing lines—has fed on honey-dew 'And drunk the milk of Paradise'. If such a poet were to build a dome, some readers argue, it would be truly visionary—not simply an exquisite architectural monument but a recreation of paradise.

Whether the reader sees the poem as implying a distinction between Kubla's dome and the poet's depends upon his reading of two ambiguous lines, 45–6. Is the poet planning to build a material dome reaching high *into* the air, *inspired* by music? Or would his be an unearthly dome, of pure harmony? The latter would be a 'miracle', the former a 'device': those two words (lines 35) encapsulate the ambiguity at the heart of the poem.

The dejection poems

Although these two poems are basically on the same subject, and one of them includes the other, there are distinct thematic differences, and they are formally quite different. One is a long confessional lyric poem; the other is one of the most perfect examples of the Romantic ode. The ode may be defined as the most formally complex kind of lyric poetry. Traditionally it is reserved for the most serious and intense expressions of feeling on public or philosophical themes. English poets have modelled their odes on those of Horace (Latin poet, 65–8BC) and Pindar (Greek poet, 522–442BC). The Horatian ode, of which Coleridge's 'Ode to Tranquillity' and Shelley's 'Ode to the West Wind' are examples, is constructed of regular stanzas. The Pindaric ode is more complicated. Originally intended to be chanted by a chorus, it uses lines of varying length and metre arranged in sections (strophe, antistrophe and epode). Earlier English poets attempted to follow Pindar's model very closely, even imitating his Greek metres, but by Coleridge's time a more flexible form had developed—still elevated and dignified, but allowing a free variation of metrical effects. Of this 'greater ode', Wordsworth's 'Ode:

Intimations of Immortality' and Coleridge's answering poem, 'Dejection: an Ode', are the finest examples. Coleridge uses couplets and quatrain rhyme schemes, lines of varying length (from six to twelve syllables), masculine and feminine rhymes, and a variety of metres, to add vitality—a sense of sweep and eventfulness—to the verse. His handling of the shorter lines should be noticed especially: they are used either for effects of delicacy (121–2) or to isolate a line of particular emotional force (as in line 8).

Both poems are dated 4 April 1802. The usual view is that Coleridge first wrote the verse letter, and then edited from it the shorter ode, reducing 340 lines to 139, at a later date. The ode is seen as a censored version, more perfectly composed but less sincere. Whereas the published ode blames his failing creativity on 'abstruse research' and a declining capacity for joy, the longer poem appears to blame Sara Coleridge for driving him to that 'abstruse research', and associates his loss of joy with his hopeless love for Sara Hutchinson. This view has been challenged, however. George Dekker asks whether it is probable that so perfect an ode could be produced merely by cutting and rearranging a longer poem.*. He argues that long before 4 April 1802 Coleridge had been working on a version of the ode, and that both the letter and the ode are based on that earlier material. He also suggests that the ode is in some ways the more accurate poem, in that the letter, although more personal, is also more self-pitying. To produce the letter Coleridge used some existing stanzas of poetry, interwoven with more spontaneous passages (in verse of much rougher quality) to make a personal version for Sara Hutchinson and a few other friends.

Such information does not necessarily make one prefer one version to the other. Formally, the letter, with its extra lines, does not seem to have the unity or the dramatic power of the ode. For instance, its use of the 'wind-harp' image is less prominent, and the primary themes are slightly obscured by so much autobiographical musing. Yet, if a reader values poetry for its confessional quality, the letter is certainly richer, and it is valued more highly by many readers for that reason.

A remark in Coleridge's *Philosophical Lectures* helps to explain why, in these poems, he associates poetic genius and joy. 'In joy individuality is lost and it therefore is liveliest in youth', before the hardships of life make men self-centred.

> To have a genius is to live in the universal, to know no self but that which is reflected not only from ... our fellow creatures ... but from the flowers, the beasts, yea from the very surface of the waters and the sands of the desert. A man of genius finds a reflex to himself, were it only in the mystery of being.

* Dekker, G., *Coleridge and the Literature of Sensibility*, Vision Press, London, 1978.

Genius and Joy are interdependent; both imply participation in the divine harmony of life. The doctrine of these poems is clarified by this comment. In the poetry there appears to be a contradiction between the thought that joy is *given*, and the thought that 'we receive but what we give/And in our life alone does Nature live'. A reader could reasonably be expected to understand the latter to mean that the life of nature is a mere projection of the mind, and the beauty of nature is simply a reflection of the soul. The key is to see that what conditions the 'gift' of joy is a response to 'the mystery of being', a power of reciprocating: one cannot receive if one does not give, but that does not invalidate the 'gift'. Similarly, nature does of course 'live', but is only *felt* to do so by those whose lives are responsive—who do not, whether in grief, dejection, or the exercise of merely scientific understanding, cut themselves off from union.

In both poems there is of course the paradox that Coleridge is mourning the loss of his 'genial' spirits in a poem which demonstrates high powers of creativity. He also claims not to feel the beauty which he so beautifully evokes in the opening lines. Given his theme, he has a tactical problem: he must make *us* feel what he has lost, while suggesting his own detachment. How do the first fifty lines of the letter (lines 1–46 of the ode) do this?

The most imaginative observation in the opening passage is the one quoted from the ballad. Coleridge's own comments tend to be descriptive rather than metaphorical, and his mind seems to wander from the present scene, wishing indeed for a different scene. His preoccupation with his own problems is to some extent reflected in the rather detached air of his description: the observations are somewhat clinical, noting the sky's 'peculiar tint of yellow green' or the 'flakes and bars' of the clouds. If you compare the detail of these lines with the sense of involvement one finds in 'This Lime-tree Bower' (lines 13–19 and 68–76), or the cluster of active images in 'Frost at Midnight' (65–74), you will probably agree that, by comparison, 'that green light that lingers in the West' has a melancholy touch. The ode's first metaphor of unity is 'wedding-garment' in line 49, and that positive note is immediately cancelled by the following 'shroud'.

There is an interesting contrast, too, between these poems and 'The Eolian Harp'. The dejection poems again make use of the harp motif. But in 'The Eolian Harp' Coleridge seemed content to imagine himself as the harp, producing music as the breeze sweeps over him. In the dejection poems he rejects this view. The true poet is not like a harp, being played by the breeze. The wind itself, which is playing the harp, is the true image for a true poet. Although in the seventh strophe of the ode there is a marked change—the long-awaited 'impulse' has arrived to change the mood—Coleridge still projects himself as the listener, not the harpist. The passage describes poetic power, both tragic and lyrical, just as the fifth strophe describes joy, and the second describes beauty. Coleridge may appreciate all three, but the closing prayer of the poem does not indicate that he participates in them himself, only that he recognises them as the most desirable of experiences. To Sara, joy and creativity may always be possible, for, unlike himself, she is blessed with a 'simple spirit' and a 'pure heart'. 'Edmund' (in the early version of the poem) is a 'lofty Poet, full of life and love'. But Coleridge, in his dejection, feels himself to be outside this harmony (and the letter shows more fully how desperate that feeling is). He even feels that perhaps he was never truly part of it: although in the past he had felt himself to be creative, perhaps it was only that 'Leaves and Fruitage, not my own, seem'd mine'. With some of the greatest poems in the language to his credit, that is clearly not the case. Nevertheless, although Coleridge went on writing poems all his life, he did not add to the body of his really superlative work.

Later poems

In 'To William Wordsworth' (1807) Coleridge achieves a marvellous recovery of poetic power to celebrate his friend's new poem. It is remarkable not least for its virtuoso presentation of a sense of inferiority:

> Ah! as I listened with a heart forlorn
> The pulses of my being beat anew:
> And even as Life returns upon the drowned,
> Life's joy rekindling roused a throng of pains
> ... Sense of past Youth, and Manhood come in vain,
> And Genius given, and Knowledge won in vain

The evocation of a 'listening heart' (95–101) is among Coleridge's most beautiful passages.

Among Coleridge's later poems the outstanding titles are probably 'Recollections of Love' (1807), 'The Visionary Hope' (1810), 'Human Life' (1815), 'To Nature' (1820), 'Work Without Hope' (1825), 'Constancy to an Ideal Object' (1826) and 'Self-Knowledge' (1832). These are, for the most part, backward-looking poems, which add to our sense of Coleridge's afflictions.

Few of them, however, are as anguished as 'The Pains of Sleep' (1803). That remarkable poem, in tense declamatory couplets, is summarised earlier. It is, in a sense, a conversation between Coleridge and his turbulent subconscious, and reveals something about his suffering. It was at about the time he wrote the poem that he sent a letter to Tom Wedgwood:

> I will not trouble you with the gloomy tale of my Health. While I am awake, by patience, employment, effort of mind, and walking I can keep the fiend at arm's length; but the night is my Hell, sleep my tormenting Angel. Three nights out of four I fall asleep, struggling to lie awake—and my frequent night-screams have almost made me a nuisance in my own house.

This is not merely about fear of nightmares. Coleridge had a deep sense of sin, and suffered acute anxiety. An entry in one of his notebooks throws light both on 'The Pains of Sleep' and on his use of the word 'dread' in the dejection poems:

> It is a most instructive part of my Life, the fact that I have always been preyed upon by some Dread, and perhaps all my faulty actions have been the consequence of some Dread or other on my mind—from fear of Pain, or Shame . . .

Coleridge's sharp sense of the nakedness of the human soul, whether in ecstacy or in anguish, is ever-present in his poetry. Without that tormented consciousness we would not have the luminous poetry of 'Frost at Midnight' or 'Kubla Khan', the purgatorial voyage of the Mariner, the lurking sense of dread in 'Christabel', or the devastating portrayal of self-alienation in 'Dejection' and 'The Pains of Sleep'. Coleridge's is a spiritual poetry, because he was a haunted spirit.

Part 4

Hints for study

IN THIS SECTION you will find suggestions for learning in an organised way, and for practising the writing of essays. You will gain nothing by merely reading this section. If you work through the exercises, they will help you to become familiar with the material. And if you work out your answers to the questions (the points you would make, and the examples you would give), you will be better prepared, when the time comes, to plan an answer quickly and effectively. Some of the questions which follow are answered in detail. Some are followed by brief notes, which you should practise expanding into essay form. Others may be answered in part by consulting earlier pages in these notes. But some can be answered only if you have studied the poems themselves attentively, and reached your own judgements concerning them.

Learning poetry

While some students find it easier to study fiction or drama, there is one great advantage in the study of poetry. It can be committed to memory. You should not necessarily learn all these poems by heart, but some of the shorter poems, and passages of the longer poems, are distinctly memorable. Once learned, they will remain with you for years, and in the process of learning them you will notice things you may have overlooked. In any case, when writing essays you should be able to quote appropriate examples to support your argument. Your quotations rhould be accurate, with the lines correctly set out, the words in the right order, and correctly punctuated. Remember that a poem is a metrical composition. Always read with the ear, not with the eye. Metre is not only an aid to memory. It is also part of the meaning.

Exercises

(1) Memorise a selection of lines from each of the poems. In these notes you will find that many passages have been treated in greater detail than others. But it is suggested that you should read through the poems slowly and carefully, selecting passages that appeal to your imagination. In the writing of essays it will help if you can recall lines which illustrate such matters as these:

(a) the variety of Coleridge's verse—the ballad metre of 'The Ancient Mariner', the conversational blank verse, the sound patterns in 'Kubla Khan', the variable line lengths in 'Dejection';
(b) key passages representing Coleridge's thought on such themes as the 'one Life', love, 'world harmony';
(c) descriptive passages—detailed natural descriptions, or those which illustrate the 'sympathy' between man and nature, or the presence of the divine in nature;
(d) examples of recurring images, such as sun, moon and stars, wind and water, fountains and springs;
(e) turning-points in the poems—dramatic moments in the narrative poems, or moments of intense feeling in the lyrical poems.
(2) Familiarise yourself with a selection of Coleridge's prose statements, particularly those on the nature of poetry, the Imagination and Fancy, Reason and Understanding.
(3) Practise analysing passages of poetry in depth. Choose a passage which has not been commented on very closely in these notes (perhaps 'Dejection', lines 1–20, or 'The Ancient Mariner', lines 232–91), and write your own detailed analysis. If asked to comment on a passage in detail you should consider it at various levels. First, the context: what is the function of the passage in the poem? Then discuss the images and how they relate to Coleridge's thought (are the same images used in other poems?). Then assess how the style and form of the passage contribute to the effect.
(4) To test yourself on your familiarity with the poems ask a friend to read aloud, or write down, a series of short quotations. Then try to identify the poem and context within the poem.

Questions

The first three questions below are partly answered. Question one has the most finished answer and, along with certain passages in Part 3 of these notes (for example, that on 'Romanticism' and the comparison of 'Reflections' and 'Frost at Midnight'), may be treated as a model. The answer to question two is confusingly arranged, and you should try to rearrange the material more logically. Question three is discussed rather than answered: consider how you would organise your essay.

Questions four to seven are followed by brief suggestions as to how you might answer them.

A further eight sample questions are given. Give some thought to what the questions involve. Make an essay plan, in the form of a series of points. Then develop each point into a paragraph, with appropriate examples and illustrations.

(1) Discuss the function of the Wedding-Guest in 'The Ancient Mariner'.

The first thing to be done is to establish exactly what part the Wedding-Guest actually plays in 'The Rime of the Ancient Mariner'. At the beginning of the poem the Wedding-Guest is the 'one of three' stopped by the Mariner. The last stanza concerns the effect of the Mariner's tale upon him: 'A sadder and a wiser man/He rose the morrow morn'. In between, he says very little. Yet at the beginning of the poem, he is the first to speak. He is an important guest ('and I am next of kin'), and his anger is understandable. The fact that he is unable to free himself, is dramatic evidence of the Mariner's hypnotic power. At the end of Part 1, and the beginning of Part 4, he plays a more active part: he describes the Mariner for us, and expresses the reader's anxiety at the implications of the tale. Again in Part 5 he interrupts, and is silenced by the Mariner ('I fear thee, ancient Mariner!'/Be calm thou Wedding-Guest!). In Part 7 the Mariner addresses him twice—first about his experience of loneliness ('So lonely 'twas, that God Himself/Scarce seeméd there to be'), and then in the 'moral' of the poem, 'He prayeth best who loveth best'.

It is only near the end of the poem that we are made aware that the selection of the Wedding-Guest was not accidental: 'The moment that his face I see,/I know the man that must hear me,/To him my tale I teach'. But why does the Mariner choose the Wedding-Guest? Since the scene is a wedding, the sacramental union of two people who are in love, we may conclude that the Mariner's instinct tells him that the Wedding-Guest is ignorant of the meaning of the ceremony he is attending. In the terms of the 'Dejection' ode, where wedding imagery is also used, he is one of the 'poor loveless ever-anxious crowd' and he needs instruction in the meaning of the words 'love', 'union' and 'prayer'. Perhaps the man's initial anger and impatience are signs that the Mariner's instinct was right. His listener is self-important, brusque, and lacking in charity— perhaps like the Mariner before his experience.

But the Wedding-Guest is important in another way. As listener, he represents us. It is through his eyes that we see the Mariner, not at a distance, but at arm's length; and he dramatises the emotional response which we are likely to feel at various stages of the poem. The Wedding-Guest belongs to the normal social world, to which we belong (and the fact that the meeting takes place on a literal threshold is symbolic of the threshold between normality, as we know it, and reality as the Mariner has experienced it). The more imaginatively we read, the more we have the experience of being held, ourselves, by the Mariner's 'glittering eye' and his 'skinny hand so brown'.

(2) In *Biographia Literaria* Coleridge said that his aim was to give 'human interest and a semblance of truth' to his supernatural subjects. How far does he succeed in 'The Ancient Mariner' or 'Christabel' or both?

In the same context from which the quotation comes, Coleridge speaks of trying to secure in his readers 'that willing suspension of disbelief . . . which constitutes poetic faith'. That is, he does not expect us to believe in the supernatural. Your answer should therefore concentrate on the two phrases 'human interest' and 'a semblance of truth'. In both poems we are made more interested in the central characters than in the supernatural elements themselves. In any case there is always an element of realism, even in the supernatural events. It is not impossible that one man should survive while the rest of a ship's crew dies, and in such circumstances it is perfectly credible that the survivor would experience a spiritual ordeal. Hallucinations are not uncommon in extreme situations, and the 'skeleton ship' which the Mariner sees does not have to be real to us, as long as we believe that it was real to him. Much of what follows in the poem takes place while the Mariner is unconscious.

The poem is, in any case, full of natural marvels—such as the phosphorescent sea-creatures, the celestial lights, and so on—so that the margin between natural and supernatural is lessened. In 'Christabel', although the supernatural is a significant element, many of the effects rely on suggestion only. Dogs do growl in their sleep, and embers do suddenly glow brighter in a current of air. Stronger personalities do influence weaker ones, and the fact that Christabel and Sir Leonine should both be 'enchanted' by Geraldine, and in different ways, does not strain our credulity. If Christabel's love for her dead mother can 'shield' her, which is easily believed, her fear of Geraldine may equally disturb her. In all these ways both poems have 'a semblance of truth'. (You should be able to think of further examples of this kind).

The 'human interest' of the poems is also very strongly developed. From the beginning, we are interested in what happened to the Mariner because we want to know what gives him his hypnotic power over the Wedding-Guest. The story concerns suffering, and his spiritual ordeal is dealt with in terms of physical effects, and basic human needs and desires, with all of which we can sympathise. There is psychological realism, too, in 'Christabel', which deals with strange events without departing from recognisable human experience, such as Christabel's fascination with the stranger, her relationship with her father, the physiological effects upon her of strong emotions, and so on.

(3) Coleridge's achievement is marked by its variety. Is variety a feature of his poetry?

This question is obscurely expressed. What do you think the questioner means by 'variety'? He could mean the various kinds of work Coleridge undertook, or his changes of opinion, or his variable temperament. The question invites you, by implication, to relate the poetry to other aspects of his life. It would be safe, therefore, to begin with a paragraph of a biographical nature, setting out the variety of Coleridge's achievement—for instance in journalism, philosophy, criticism, and poetry. And you could briefly summarise his intellectual development, or the variety of his opinions in one of these areas, pointing out, for example, how he began as a political radical and ended as a conservative theorist. But the question itself relates to the poetry, so that if you wish to write about his political or religious development you should do so with reference to the appropriate poems. The major part of your essay should deal with the variety of themes and forms in Coleridge's poems. This presents a problem of organisation. One solution is to write about particular themes, referring to the way these themes are handled in different kinds of poetry. A simpler plan would be to write about the variety of poetic forms in which Coleridge achieved excellence (the ode, the conversation poem, the ballad) and to illustrate the nature of his achievement within each form.

(4) In what ways are 'Frost at Midnight' and 'Kubla Khan' both Romantic poems?

Your answer should include: a brief definition of the term Romantic; an appreciation of each poem, calling attention to major themes; a comparison of the two poems (considering the strong feeling in both, the expression of visionary hope, and so on); a contrast of the two poems (the setting, form and style); and a conclusion.

(5) Coleridge distinguished between 'form', which develops organically from the content of a poem, and 'shape' which is imposed on the content of a poem. How do his poems demonstrate a preference for organic form?

An answer to this question could consider the evolution of the conversation poems, the form of both dejection poems (when compared with more formal lyrics) and the structure of the ballad poems.

(6) How do Coleridge's poems reflect 'the spirit of divinest liberty'?

Consider the meaning of 'liberty' in the poem from which the quotation is taken, and compare it with Coleridge's treatment of the theme in 'The Dungeon', 'Fears in Solitude' and 'Frost at Midnight'.

(7) Coleridge said that the poet should be aloof from his own feelings. Is this true of his own poetry?

Beware: there is a distinction between being 'aloof' from one's feelings and being without feelings. The former implies the ability to contemplate one's own feelings clearly, almost as if they were another's. Without this ability a poet could not interest us in his feelings. You could answer this question with reference to 'The River Otter', 'The Ancient Mariner', 'Reflections', 'This Lime-tree Bower' and other poems.

Further sample questions

(1) One of the features of Romanticism is said to be a fascination with the past. Is this true of Coleridge's poetry?

(2) Compare and contrast 'Dejection: an Ode' and 'A Letter to Sara Hutchinson'.

(3) Why are the 'conversation poems' so called?

(4) The Romantics were idealists. But they wrote their finest poems about disillusionment. Discuss.

(5) Which of Coleridge's poems appeals to you most? Why?

(6) Write an essay on Coleridge as a poet of nature.

(7) To what extent does one need a knowledge of philosophy to appreciate Coleridge's poetry?

(8) Write an essay on *either* the theme of friendship *or* the sense of place in Coleridge's poetry.

Part 5

Suggestions for further reading

The texts

Coleridge: Poetical Works, edited by E.H. Coleridge, Oxford University Press, London, 1969. This is a one-volume paperback edition of the poems, using the text of the standard two-volume edition *The Complete Poetical Works of S.T. Coleridge*, Oxford University Press, Oxford, 1912. The verse Letter is not included.
Biographia Literaria, edited by J. Shawcross, two volumes, Oxford University Press, Oxford, 1907.
Coleridge's Poems, edited by John Beer, Everyman's Library, J. M. Dent & Sons Ltd, London and New York, 1974. A very full selection, arranged in chronological sections, with an introduction to each phase of Coleridge's work. If possible, use this edition for your studies. It is the one used in the compilation of these notes.
The Portable Coleridge, edited by I.A. Richards, The Viking Press, New York, 1950, and Penguin Books, Harmondsworth, 1977. A shorter selection of poems, but including a useful selection from the letters and prose works.

Biography

BATE, W.J.: *Coleridge*, Weidenfeld and Nicolson, London, 1969.

Criticism

ABRAMS, M.H. (ED.): *English Romantic Poets*, 2nd edition, Oxford University Press, Oxford and London, 1975. Contains four good essays on Coleridge's poems.
BEER, JOHN: *Coleridge the Visionary*, Chatto and Windus, London, 1959. A study of Coleridge's poetry in the context of religious thought.
COBURN KATHLEEN, (ED.): *Coleridge: A Collection of Critical Essays*, Twentieth Century Views, Prentice-Hall, New Jersey, 1967. The widest selection of essays. It includes A.S. Gerard's influential essay 'The Systolic Rhythm: the structure of Coleridge's Conversation Poems'.

GRANT, ALLAN: *A Preface to Coleridge,* Longman, London, 1972. An illustrated introduction, especially useful for its reference section.

HOLMES, RICHARD: *Coleridge,* Past Masters, Oxford University Press, Oxford, 1982. An admirable short study of Coleridge as writer and thinker.

HOUSE, A.H.: *Coleridge,* Hart-Davis, London, 1953. A general critical study.

JONES, ALUN R., and WILLIAM TYDEMAN, (EDS.): *Coleridge: The Ancient Mariner and Other Poems,* Casebook Series, Macmillan, London, 1973. Reprints important essays by George Whalley and Edward E. Bostetter on 'The Ancient Mariner'

SCHULZ, MAX F.: *The Poetic Voices of Coleridge,* Wayne State University Press, Detroit, 1963. Sophisticated modern criticism of the range and variety of Coleridge's poetry.

WALSH, WILLIAM: *Coleridge: the Work and the Relevance,* Chatto and Windus, London, 1967. A clear exposition of Coleridge's ideas.

WARREN, ROBERT PENN: 'A poem of Pure Imagination,' in *Selected Essays,* Eyre and Spottiswoode, London, 1964. A classic essay on 'The Ancient Mariner'.

WILLEY, BASIL: *Samuel Taylor Coleridge,* Chatto and Windus, London, 1972. A study of Coleridge's philosophical and religious work. See also the same writer's chapter on Coleridge in *Nineteenth Century Studies,* Chatto and Windus, 1949.

YARLOTT, GEOFFREY: *Coleridge and the Abyssinian Maid,* Methuen, London, 1967. Readable criticism allied to biographical interest.

If your time is limited, the most useful of the above books are Kathleen Coburn's critical anthology and W.J. Bate's critical biography.

The author of these notes

RICHARD GRAVIL studied at the universities of Wales, Bristol and East Anglia. He taught at the University of Victoria in Canada from 1964 to 1967. After doctoral research he worked first for the British Council in Japan and Tanzania, and later as reader in English Literature at the University of Lodz, Poland. Since 1980 he has been Senior Lecturer in English at The College of St Mark and St John in Plymouth.

He has edited critical anthologies on *Gulliver's Travels* and Wordsworth's *The Prelude* in the Macmillan casebook series, and co-edited two collections of critical essays on Coleridge, *Coleridge's Imagination* (1985) and *The Coleridge Connection* (1989). He has published a number of essays on Wordsworth, Conrad, Lawrence, and contemporary poetry, and is author of the York Notes on *Gullivers Travels*.